Bristol **Safari**

In search of the **city's urban wildlife**

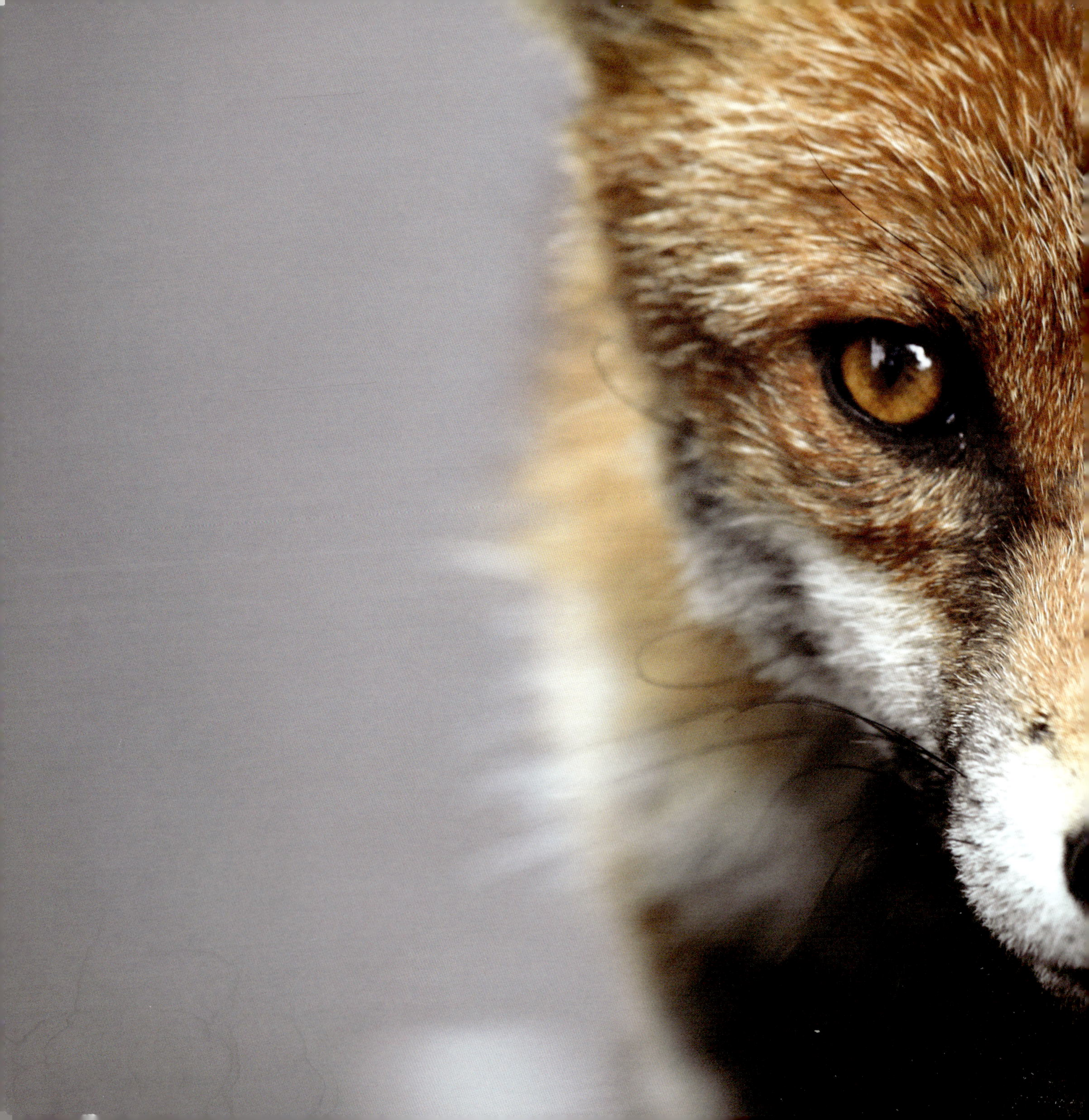

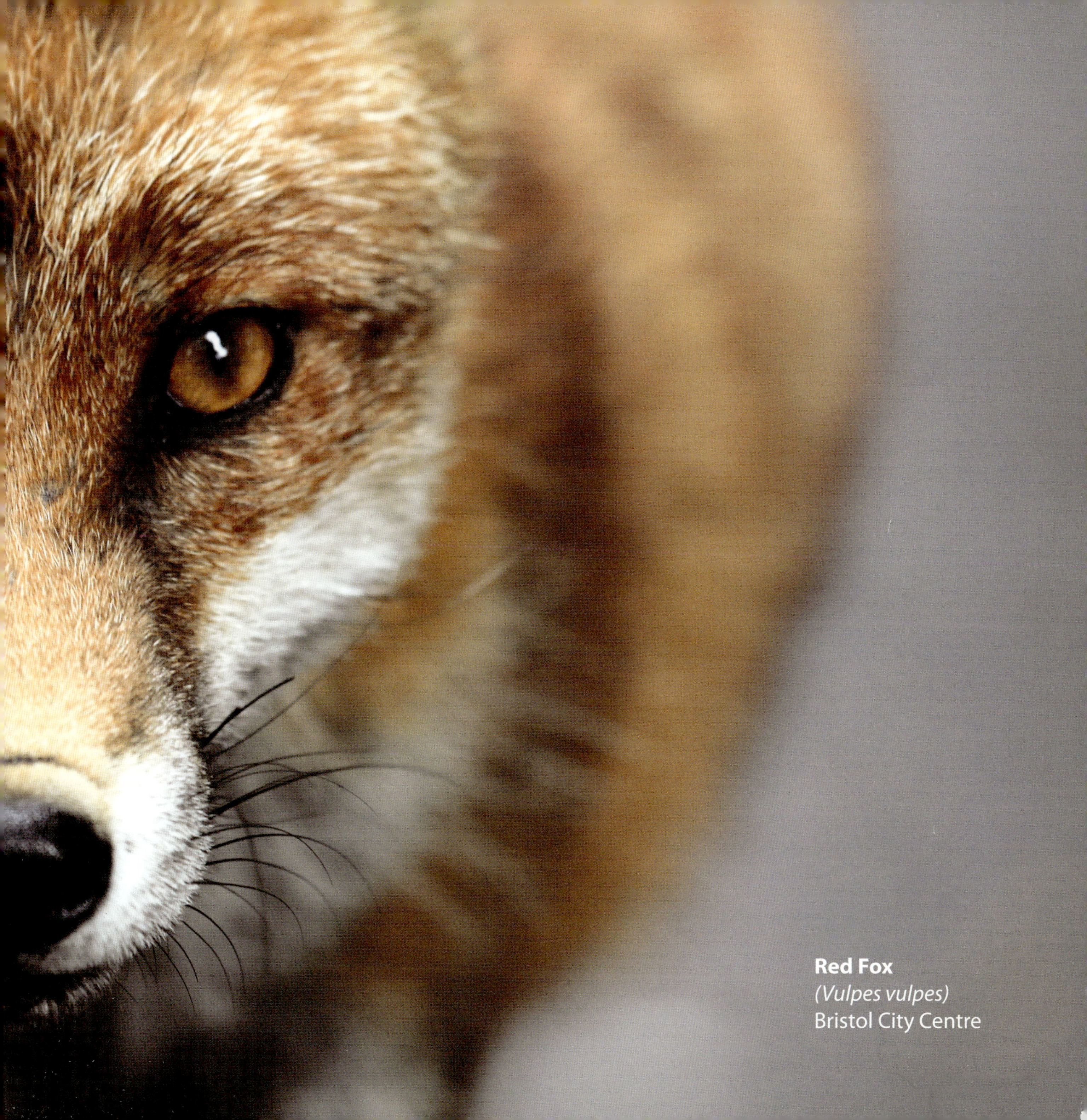

Red Fox
(Vulpes vulpes)
Bristol City Centre

I dedicate this book

to my parents

they are my **heroes**

I would also like to give a big thank you to Steve Micklewright, Director of Avon Wildlife Trust, for all his help on this project and for his tireless work in Bristol fighting for green spaces. Also I would like to thank John Sansom of Redcliffe Press for letting me have a shot at putting a book together. To Farrah Chandra Senthi for all her support on this project. Finally Freddy The Fox for letting me into his world for a magical five months.

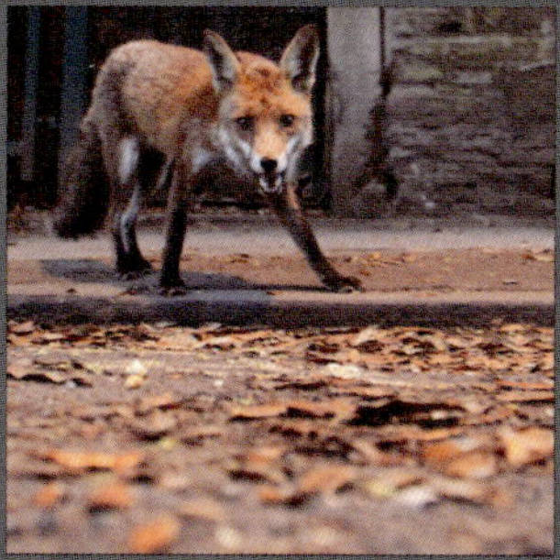

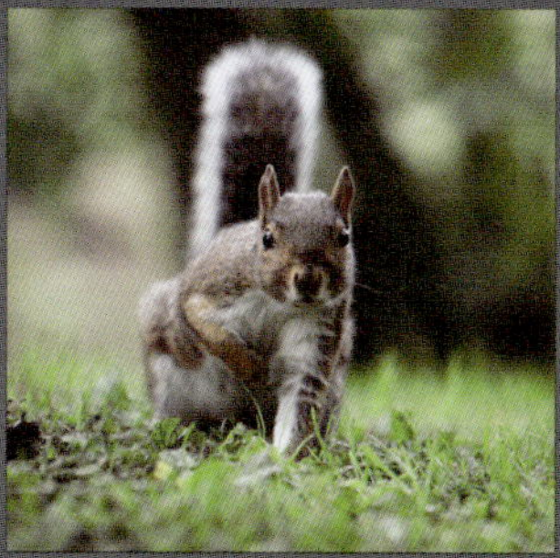

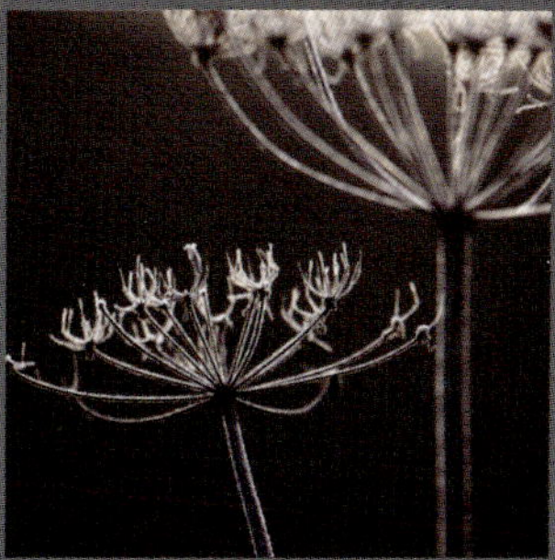

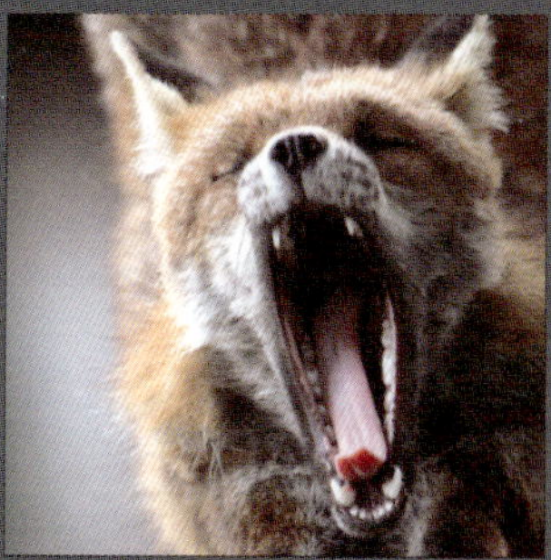

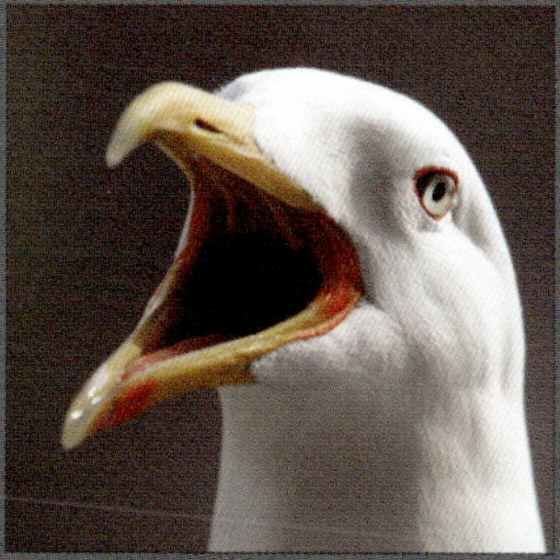

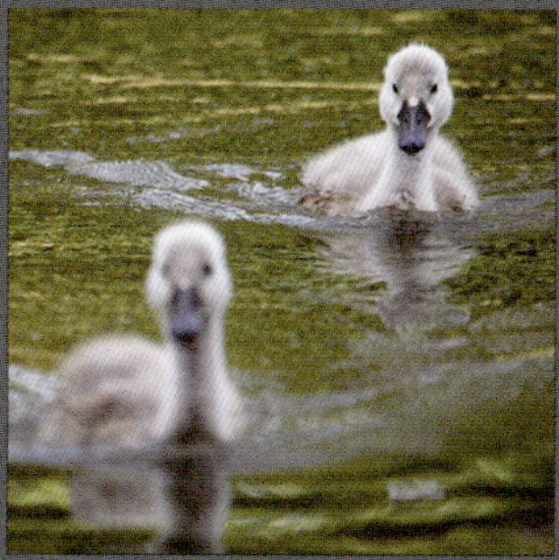

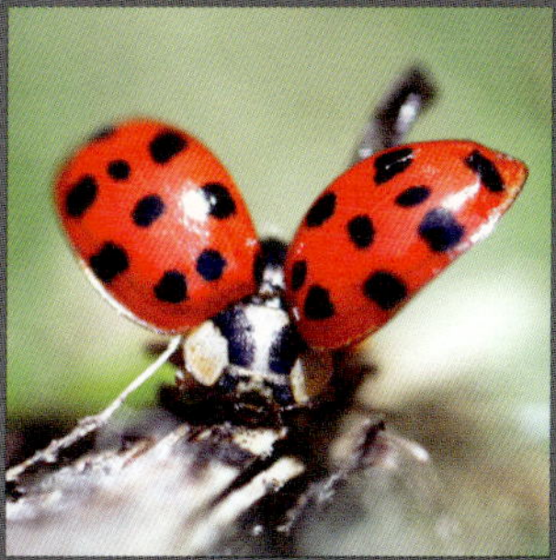

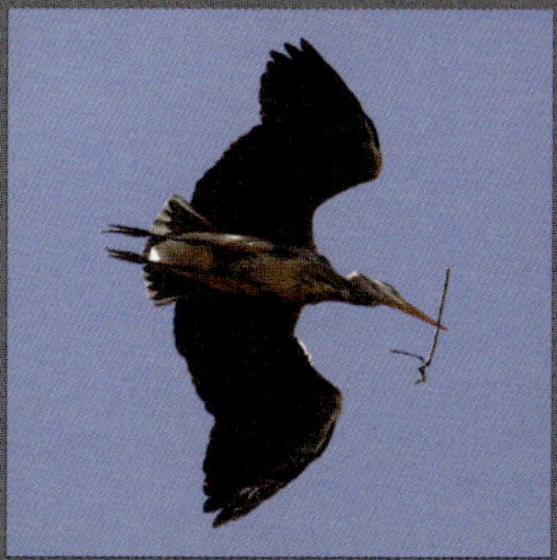

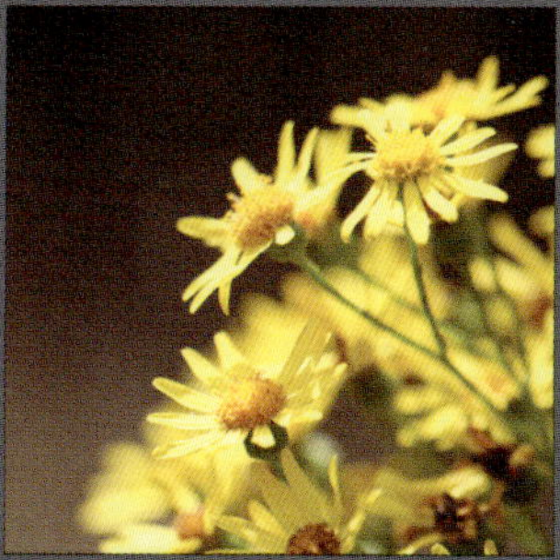

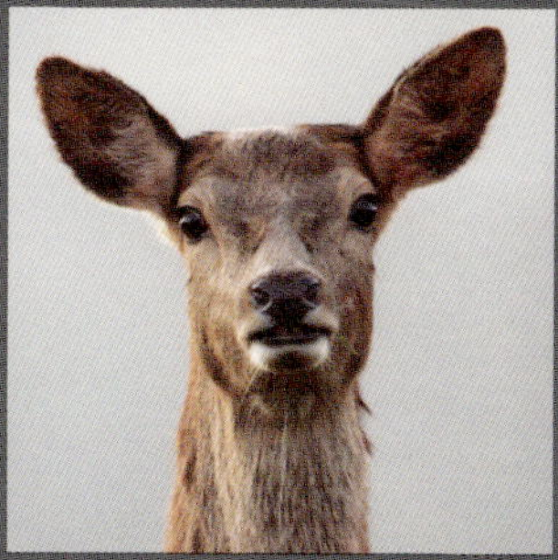

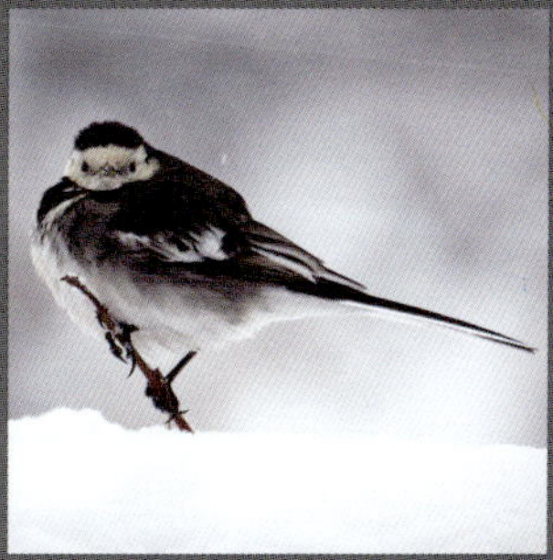

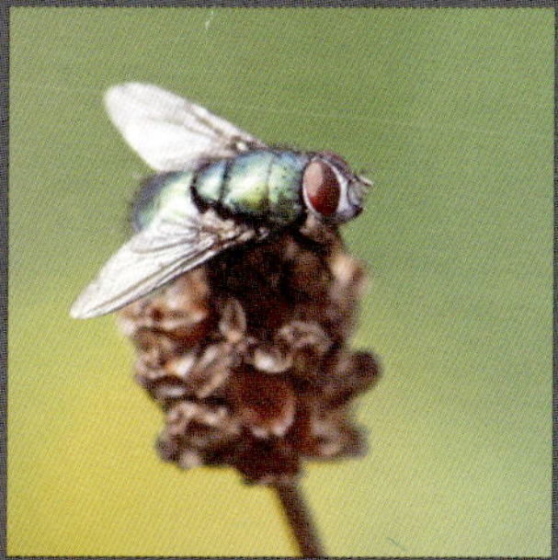

Bristol **Safari**
In search of the **city's urban wildlife**

Ian Wade

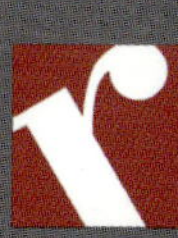

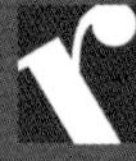

First published in 2011 by Redcliffe Press Ltd.,
81g Pembroke Road, Bristol BS8 3EA

www.redcliffepress.co.uk
info@redcliffepress.co.uk

© Ian Wade

ISBN   978-1-906593-89-6

British Library Cataloguing-in-Publication Data
A catalogue record for this book is available from the British Library

Design and typesetting by Ian Wade
Printed by HSW, Tonypandy, Rhondda

Contents

8   Foreword

9   Introduction

11   A bit about me

12   Bristol Docks and Floating Harbour

24   Brandon Hill Nature Reserve

40   Eastville Park, Snuff Mills and Oldbury Court Estate

52   Urban Foxes Cotham

68   Bedminster Down

72   Downs and the Avon Gorge

78   Ashton Court Estate

82   Bishopsworth

84   Bristol City Centre and Stokes Croft

91   Avon Wildlife Trust

92   Arnos Vale Cemetery

Foreword

Bristol is alive with wildlife. Whether you are in the heart of the city or walking in those special places that feel like they are in the countryside, you are never far away from a wild creature. This wonderful book illustrates that perfectly. Who would have thought that the streets of Cotham are home to some of the most easily seen foxes or that the parkland along the River Frome is where you can hear tawny owls hooting at night? But this book shows that it is not just the more charismatic species we should be looking out for. Almost everywhere you go you will find wildlife going about its business. Whether it's spiders building traps in walls or sea gulls scavenging from waste bins, there is always something to see.

I really hope Ian Wade's book will inspire you to visit some of Bristol's special places for wildlife and that it might encourage you to do your bit to protect it too. Even planting a few plants for bees and butterflies in a window box would help. But there is much more you can do too - just visit http://www.avonwildlifetrust.org.uk to find out.

Steve Micklewright
Director
Avon Wildlife Trust

Introduction

Most people think you have to travel to far-off lands like the Masai Mara in Africa or the tropical rain forests of Malaysia to experience truly exciting wildlife and take great pictures. Closer to home, people living in the city head out into the British countryside to photograph wild animals while right under their noses is a world of diverse and intriguing flora and fauna. Indeed, much of the wildlife we photograph and enjoy in the countryside is often easier to see in our cities and towns. This is because some creatures are well-adapted to the opportunities offered by city life, like foxes. Others have moved into the city in recent years, like magpies, while the city has grown around colonies of other creatures, especially badgers. Meanwhile, many of the natural habitats of these creatures have been lost from the countryside.

British urban environments are just as exciting as our green countryside. Instead of thick woodland canopies and fields we have concrete platforms, streets, parks and town centres – all offering animals homes and places to feed and reproduce – offering us in turn an array of colourful creatures with different behaviours, colours and sounds. All you have to do is be patient, look that little bit harder to discover a new and exhilarating world.

Bristol is famous for its art and architecture, and landmarks such as the ss Great Britain and the Clifton Suspension Bridge. But it is also a great place to see urban wildlife.
Living in Bristol we are lucky to have areas of greenery that offer environments to watch animals but some of the most exciting locations are right in the centre of the busy city, sometimes in our own gardens or even under our garden sheds!

This book is my personal photographic journey through the locations I visit, photograph and enjoy daily in Bristol. In these pages, we will visit locations like the Bristol docks where you can see cormorants busily fishing for small fish and eels, or the city centre itself which comes alive after dark with creatures scavenging on the left-over food and waste we humans discard every day. I will tell you what you can expect to see, along with interesting facts and figures to make your wildlife viewing more enjoyable. Our journey will take us through Bristol's diverse wildlife from swans and their cygnets to Mediterranean spiders and unusual plants. Think of it as an urban safari. Instead of lions, giraffes and crocodiles you will see foxes, badgers and colourful insects.

So get out there and start exploring your urban safari in this most rewarding city.

Ian Wade April 2011

Myself
On the look out for kingfishers on the River Frome at Snuff Mills.

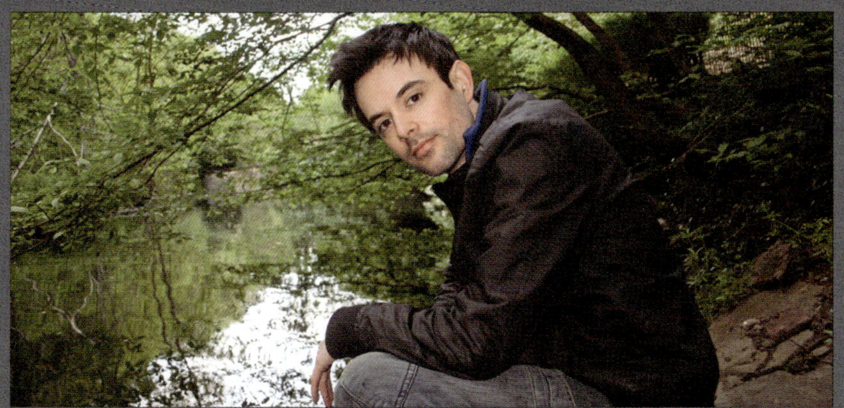

A bit about me

I suppose you could say I am obsessed with wildlife and photography. When I was a young boy I watched David Attenborough on television as millions of people did all over the world, and was mesmerised by the amazing world he revealed to us. I would sit and read books on wildlife from cover to cover every night. As I got older I wanted to find out more about the creatures. I would watch in the park, garden or on the way to work . In 2004 I bought a little compact digital camera and started photographing wildlife. My camera was basic but that didn't matter.

That was it. I was hooked. I spent all my spare time in and around Somerset photographing landscapes and wildlife. I find it hugely rewarding when you get a picture that you are proud of. I've spent the night in my car, stiff-necked from sleeping across the back seat of a Peugeot 106 – not the biggest or the most comfortable car in the world – but the whole process is worthwhile when you manage to capture that owl or badger you have been patiently waiting for. As time went on I spent more time in the city photographing wildlife and less in the country. For a couple of years I had been trying to photograph foxes in the countryside. Anybody who has tried to photograph these beautiful creatures in the wild will understand when I say they are extremely hard to watch and photograph: as soon as you make a noise or they catch your scent they are off. Urban foxes act completely differently. They hang around and check you out, even sometimes follow you home! This enables us to experience a wild animal at close quarters – something which is very rare in the countryside.

Watching wildlife in the city I have found myself on a massive learning curve but that's what I find exciting. There is so much more to see and learn.

www.ianwadephotography.co.uk

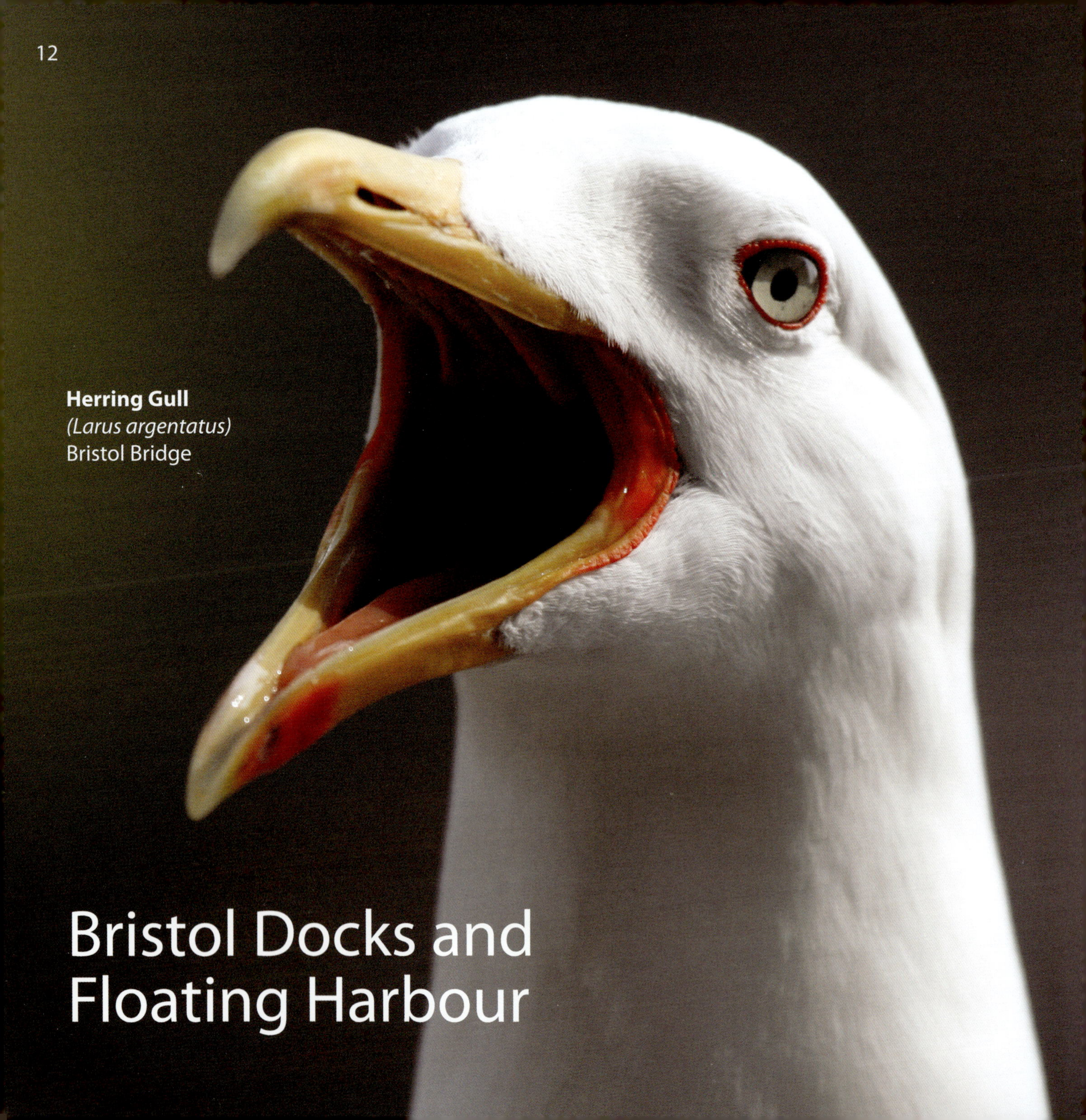

Herring Gull
(Larus argentatus)
Bristol Bridge

Bristol Docks and Floating Harbour

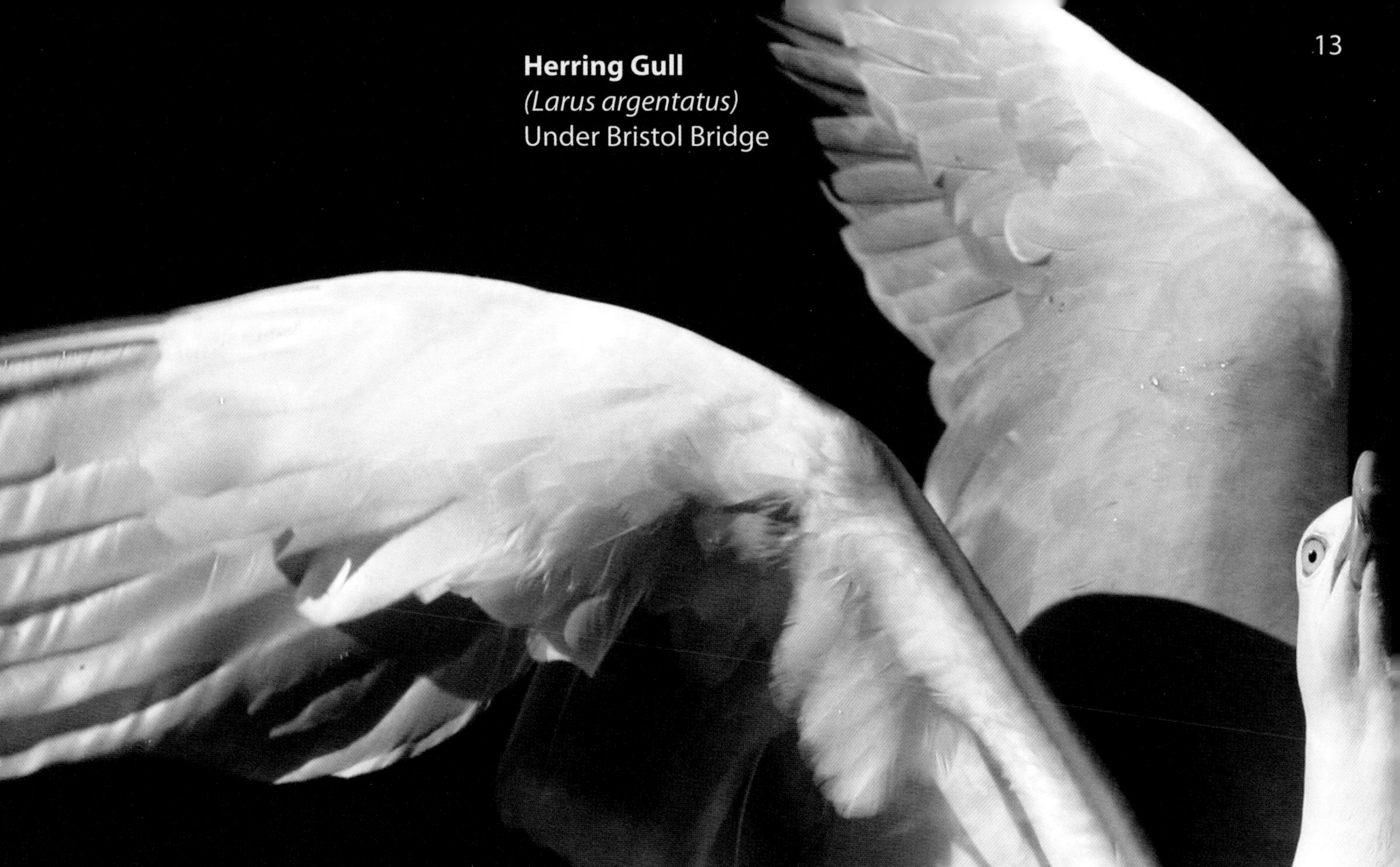

Bristol's harbour is now a tourist attraction with warehouses and dockside buildings converted to museums, galleries, exhibitions, bars and night-clubs. Surprisingly, in this sophisticated environment, the area is an exciting place to watch and enjoy Bristol's wildlife. Prominent are what most of us group together as 'seagulls' – the herring gulls and lesser black-backed gulls.

The herring gulls are one of the largest birds you will see in Bristol. They get a bad press from local residents especially in July and August when they get aggressive and noisy after young have hatched. During the summer an astonishing 2,000 pairs of herring and lesser black-backed gulls nest in Bristol. They use the Floating Harbour for washing, feeding and resting. Before the 1970s, gulls didn't nest in Bristol. Since then rubbish tips have provided a great source of food.

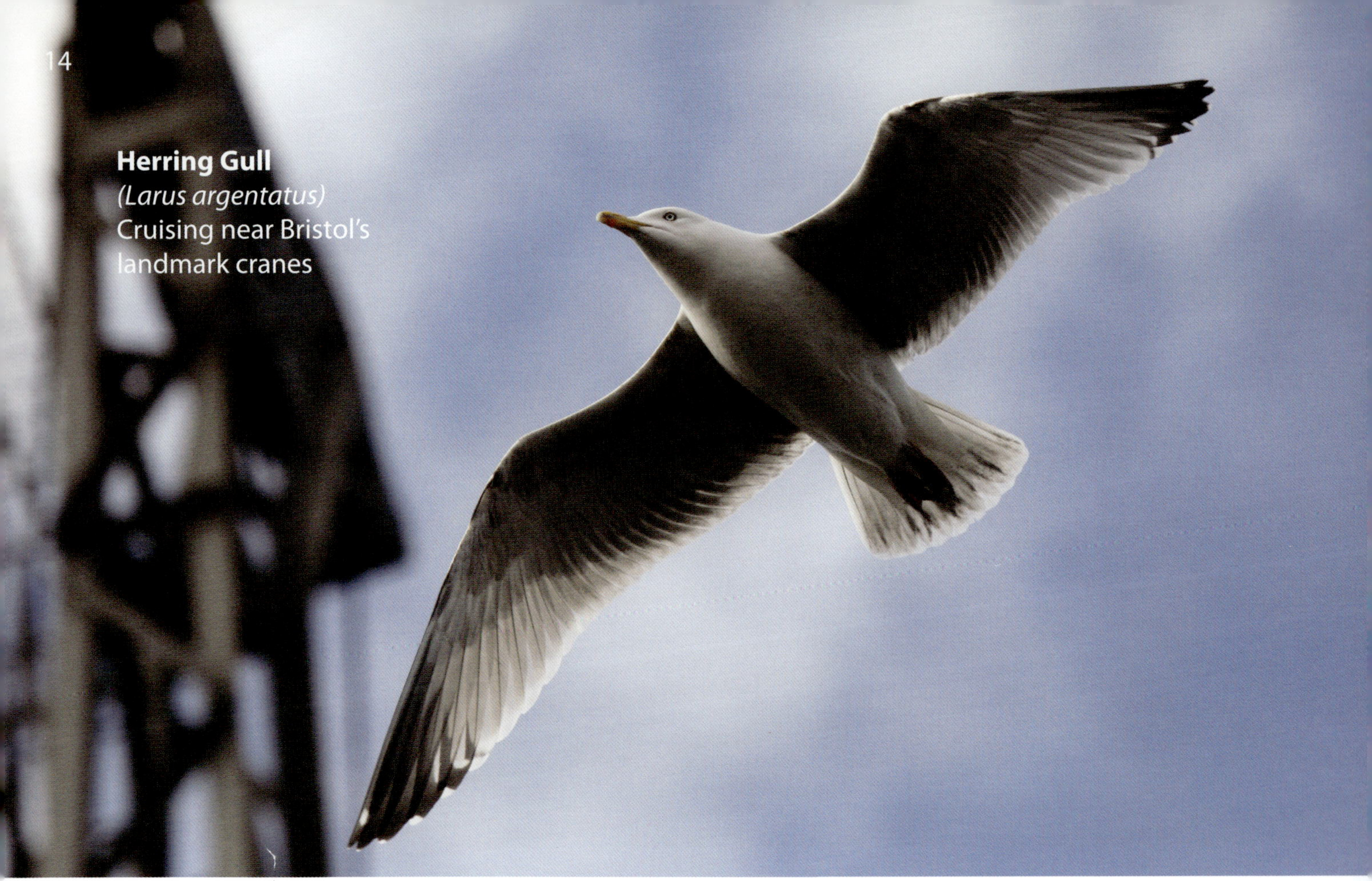

Herring Gull
(Larus argentatus)
Cruising near Bristol's landmark cranes

The gulls can be identified by the colour of their legs. The black-headed are red, the lesser black-backed are yellow, while herring gulls are pink. There's a strong chance you'll see Britain's smallest gull – the black-headed gull.

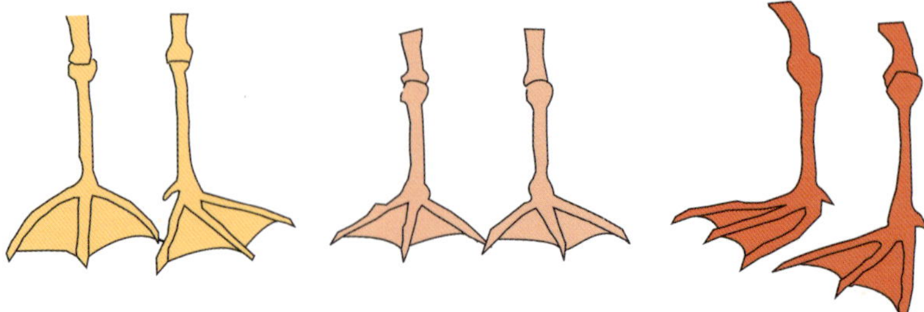

Left to right: Lesser black-backed gull; Herring gull; Black-headed gull

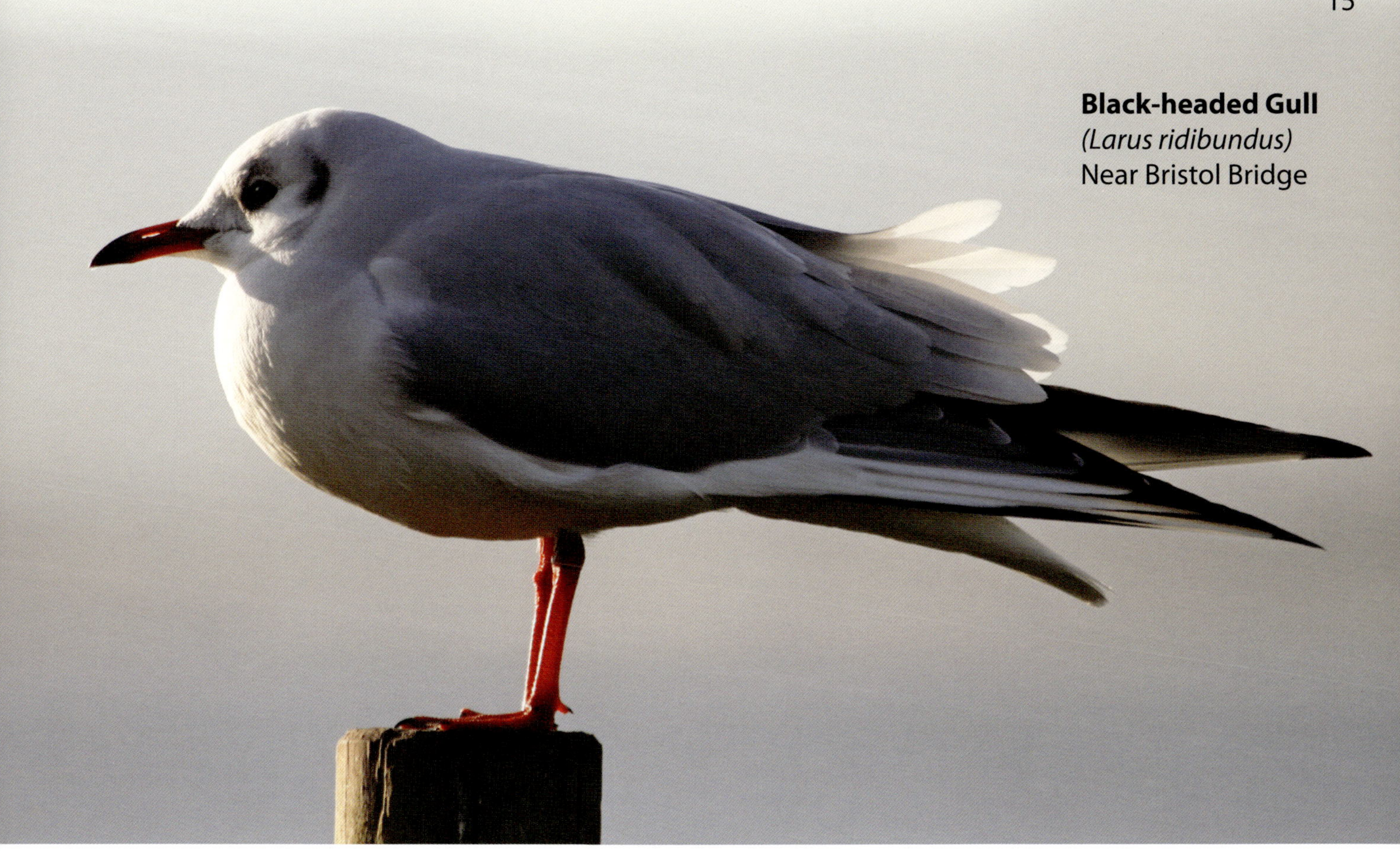

Black-headed Gull
(Larus ridibundus)
Near Bristol Bridge

There are reckoned to be 500 or more in central Bristol. They commute to the city daily from Chew Valley Lake in search of food. During the summer the black-headed gull has a chocolate brown hood. In the winter this disappears and is replaced by a dark spot behind its eye. Another bird sharing this area, and one of my favourites, is the cormorant. This is a truly fascinating bird to watch around the harbour area.

Great swimmers, cormorants float low, often showing only their head and neck above water. In a characteristic movement, they dive by jumping up and plunging head-first into the water. But sometimes they simply sink. The longest recorded dive is more than a full minute, perhaps to a depth of 100 feet. Swimming 20 feet or so beneath the surface, they tend to stay submerged for less than 30 seconds.

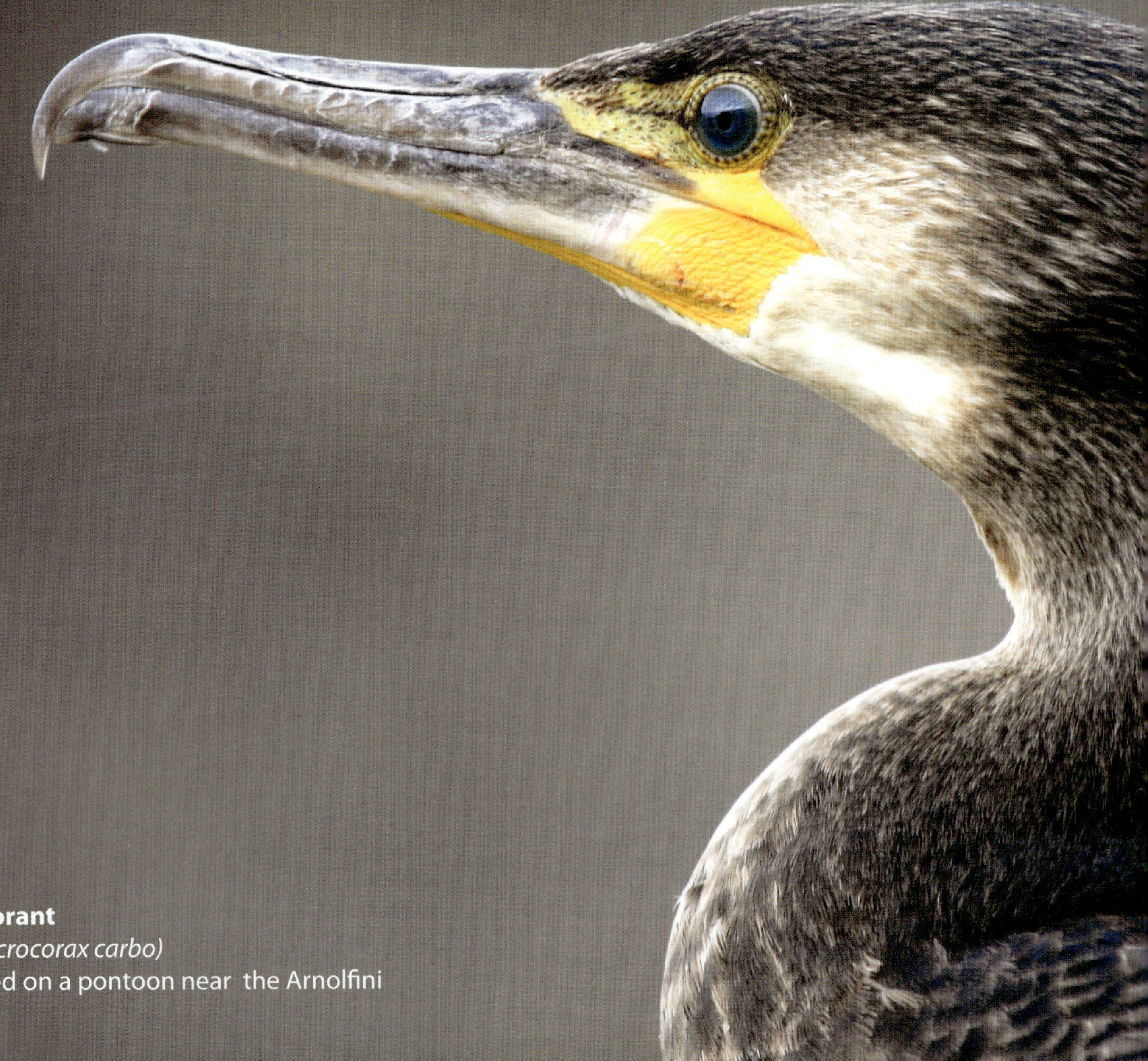

Cormorant
(Phalacrocorax carbo)
Perched on a pontoon near the Arnolfini

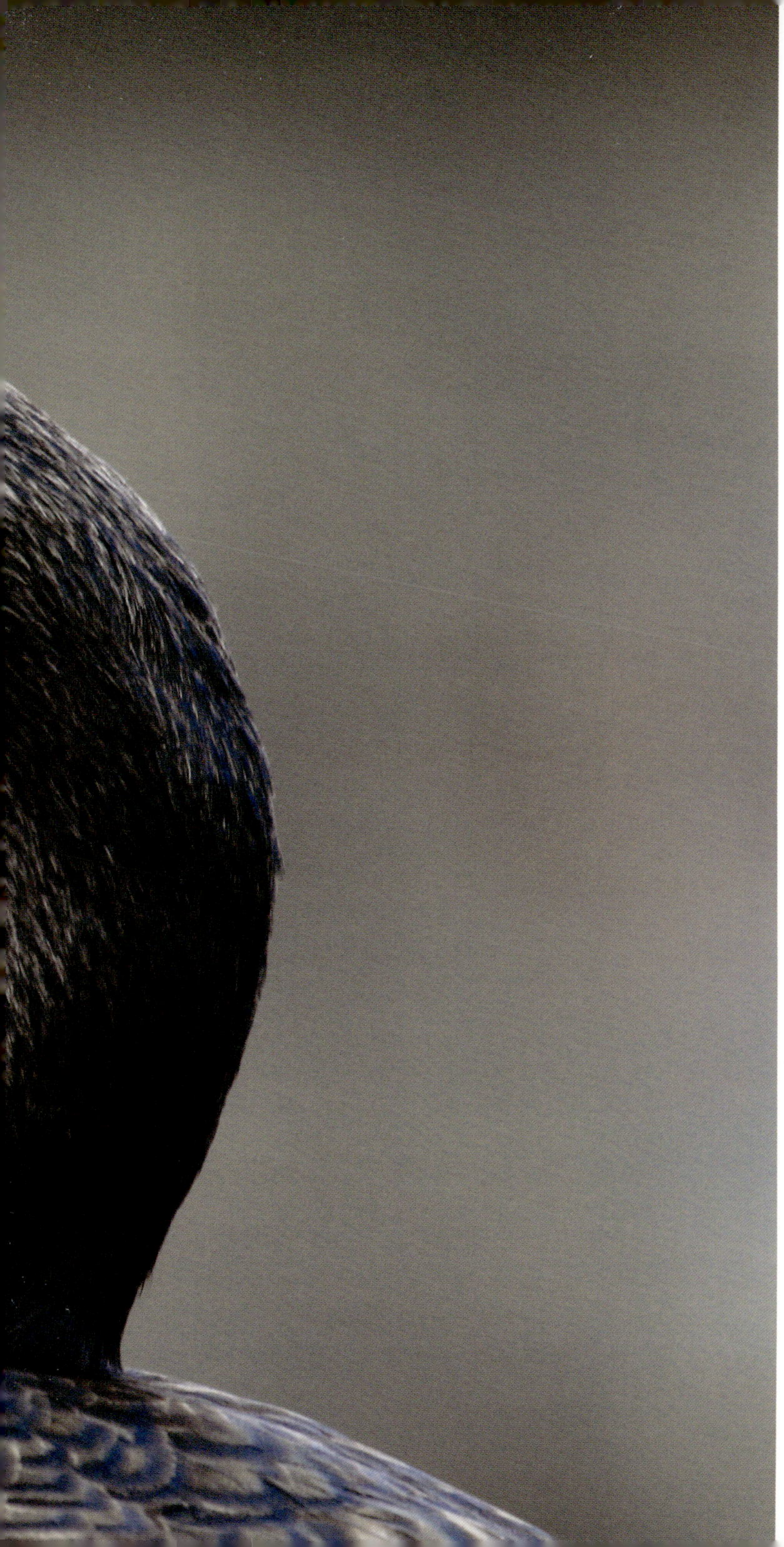

After fishing they rest on the jetties and buildings, often holding their wings out to dry. They do this because they are less waterproof than ducks. Having wet feathers helps cormorants to sink and therefore dive deeper for fish and eels. The jetty below in this photograph is a popular location for cormorants. They can also be seen on pontoons near the Arnolfini. The day I took this photograph there was no sight of the cormorants, just a gentleman a little worse for wear sleeping off last night's party.

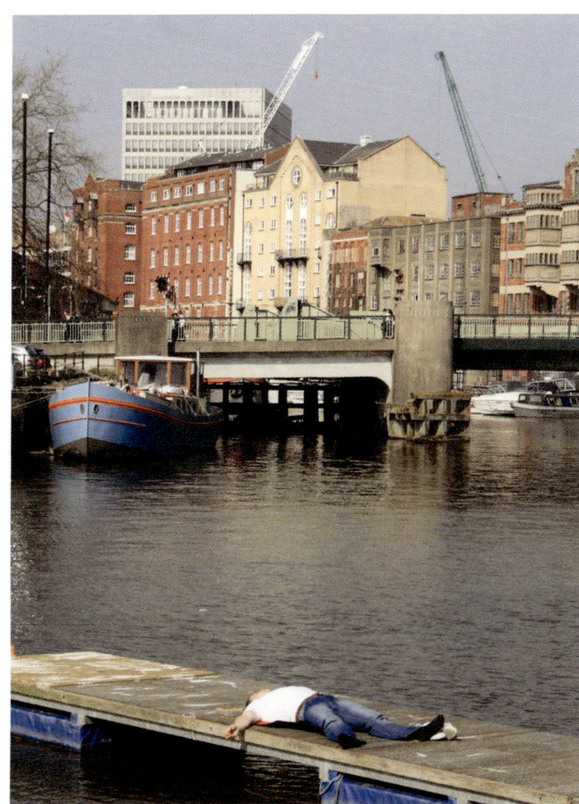

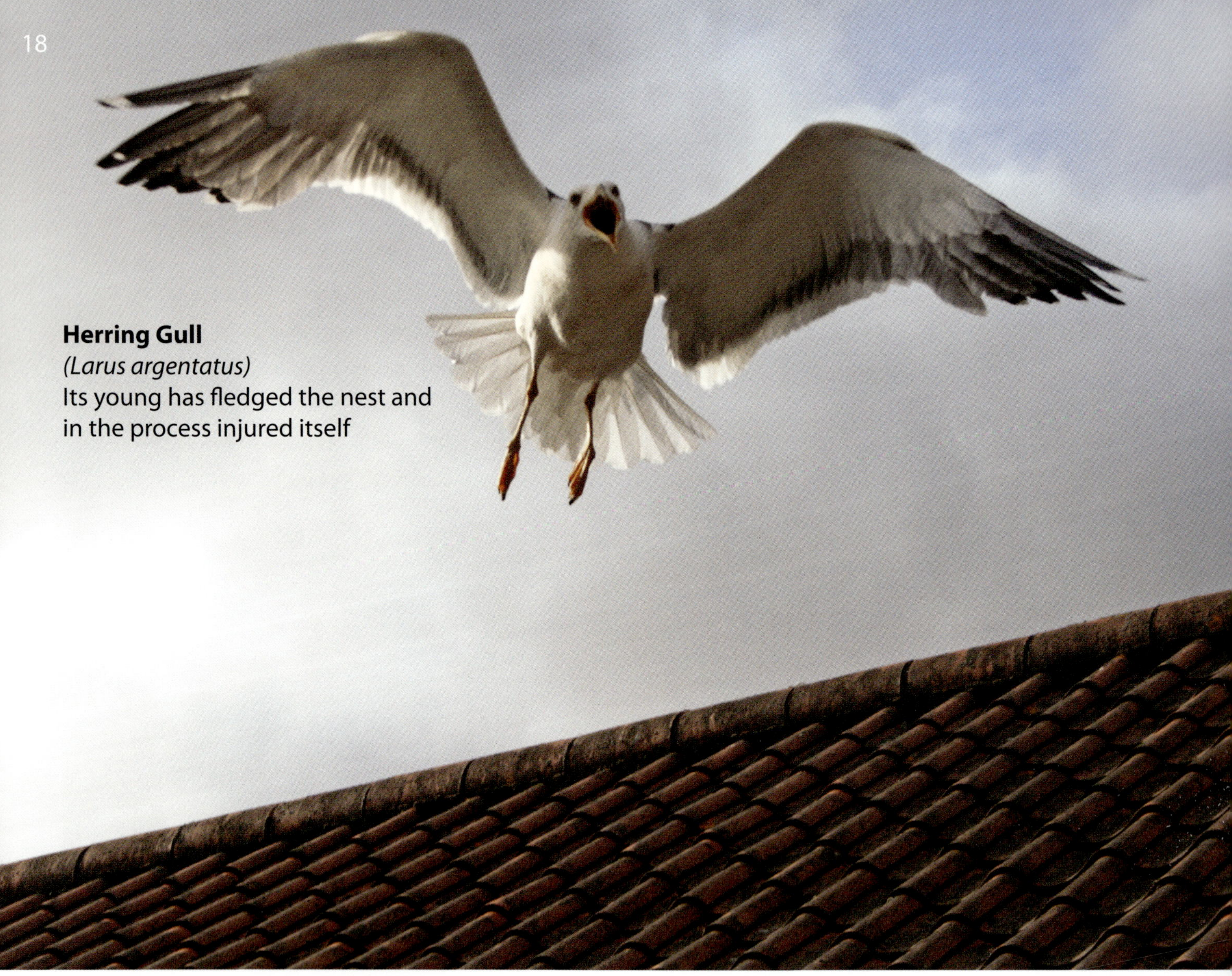

Herring Gull
(Larus argentatus)
Its young has fledged the nest and
in the process injured itself

It's always sad to see a chick which has fledged the nest and become injured. On this morning, I was walking around the harbour when I saw a juvenile bird unable to fly and limping around. The anxious parent started to attack me by dive bombing me, making a 'kyee - arrrk - warrrk - warrrk - warrrk' noise!

If a young gull can't fly or walk properly, its chances are slim. Many are picked off by cats and foxes.

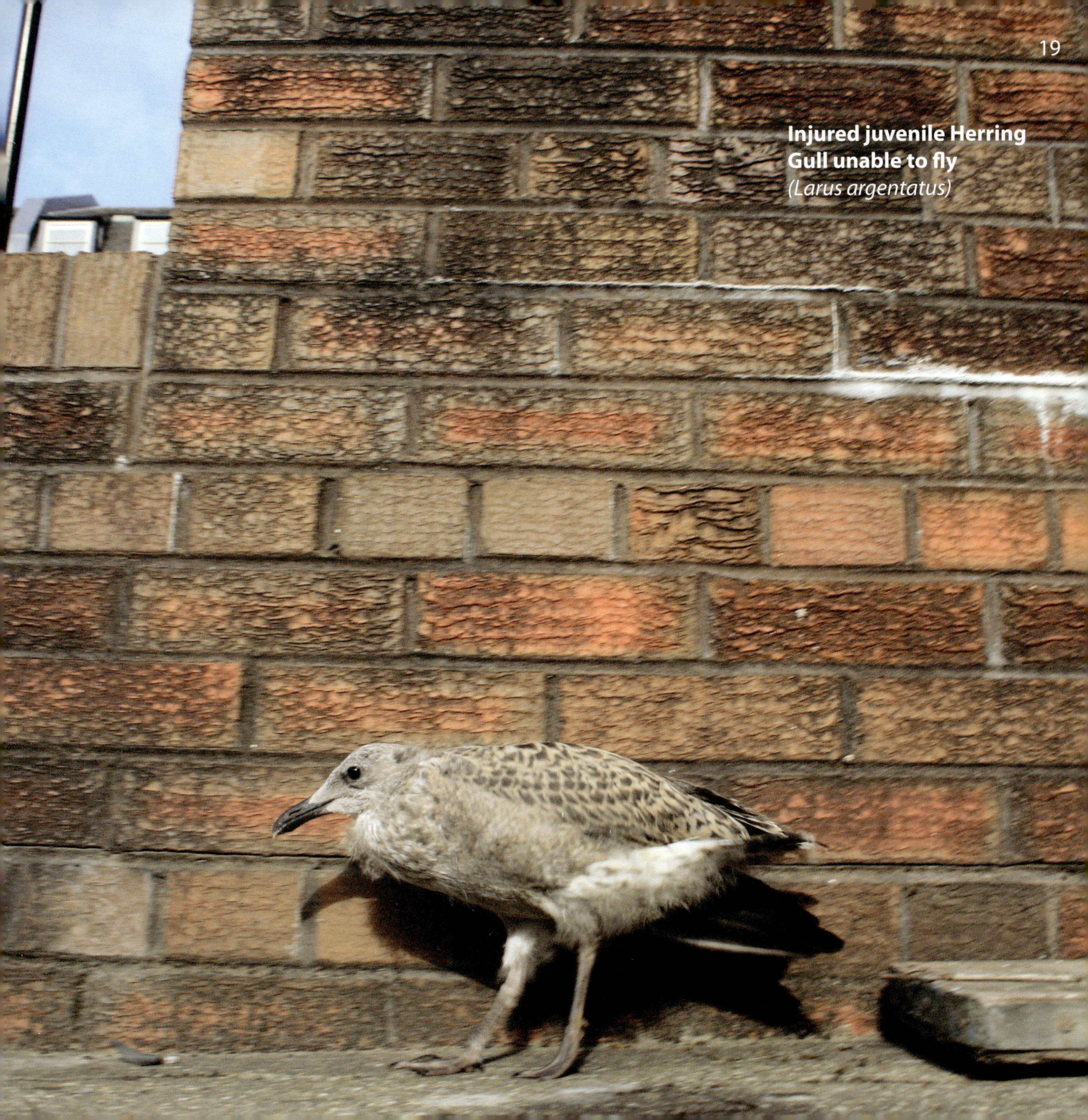

Injured juvenile Herring Gull unable to fly
(Larus argentatus)

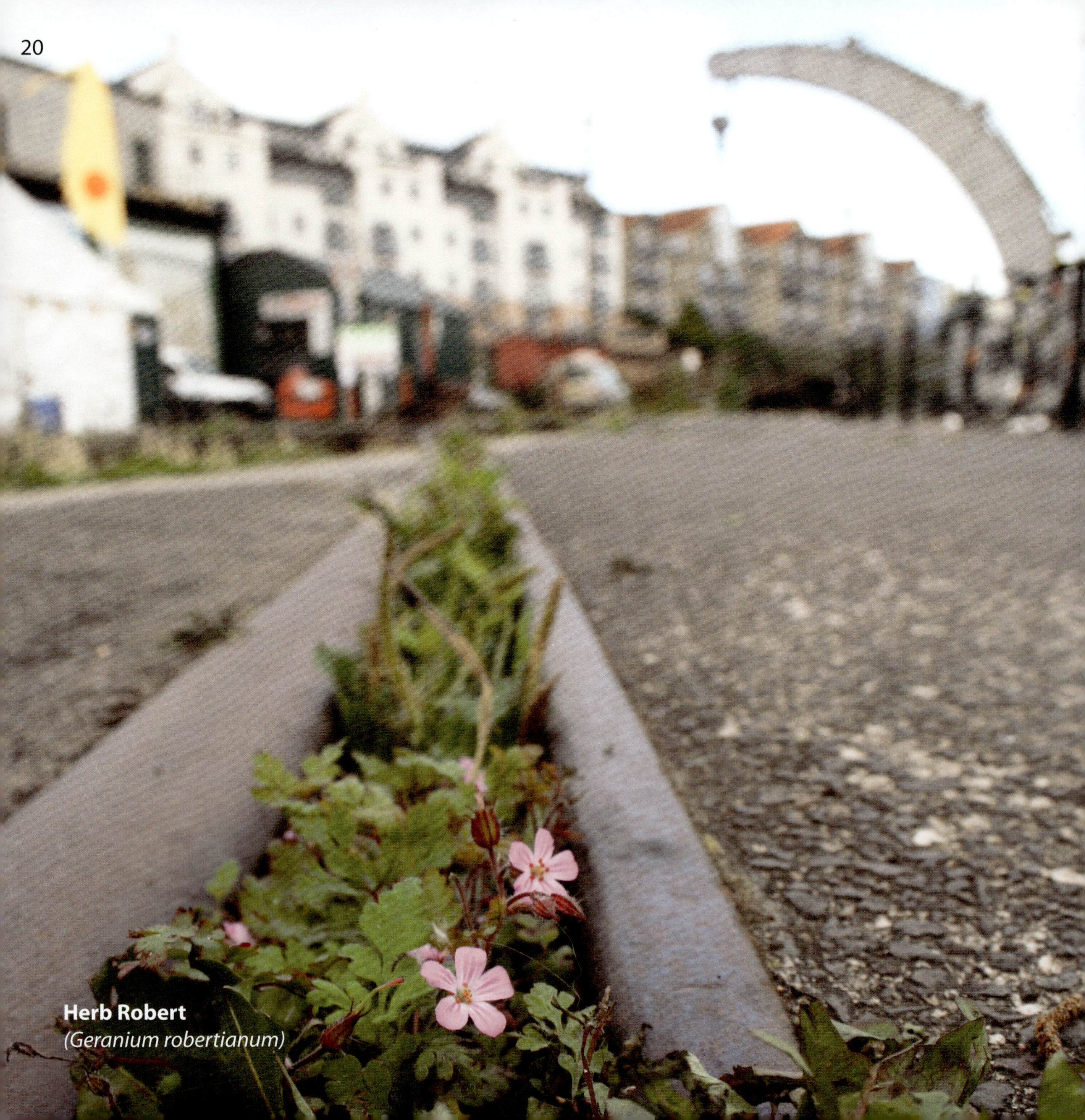
Herb Robert
(Geranium robertianum)

Most of the plants, trees and flowers found in the Floating Harbour are native to the United Kingdom but some are from further afield. Flowering plants which have taken up residence here have escaped from gardens and park areas. Their seeds have been blown in on the wind and germinated in the cracks in the concrete or holes in the stone walls. The fig trees which have become established in the harbour owe their existence to seeds from fruit tossed overboard from the many ships which have entered the harbour from foreign climes over the years. In Castle Park you can see quite large fig trees growing out of the harbour walls.

Among other plants and flowers, Mexican fleabane which originally came from Mexico looks like a pink daisy and grows in clumps in the harbour walls. During May and June keep your eye out for the bright purple bell flowers which transform the harbour walls. Other plants seen are red valerian, yellow flag iris and hemlock water dropwort. Dropwort, related to cow parsley, is a common plant in the harbour in the summer months. Warning: avoid touching this very toxic plant.

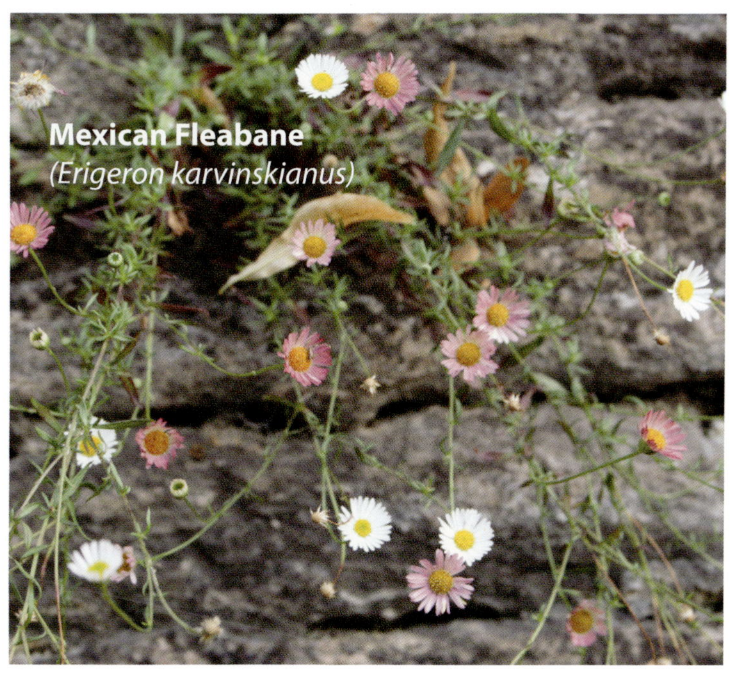

Mexican Fleabane
(*Erigeron karvinskianus*)

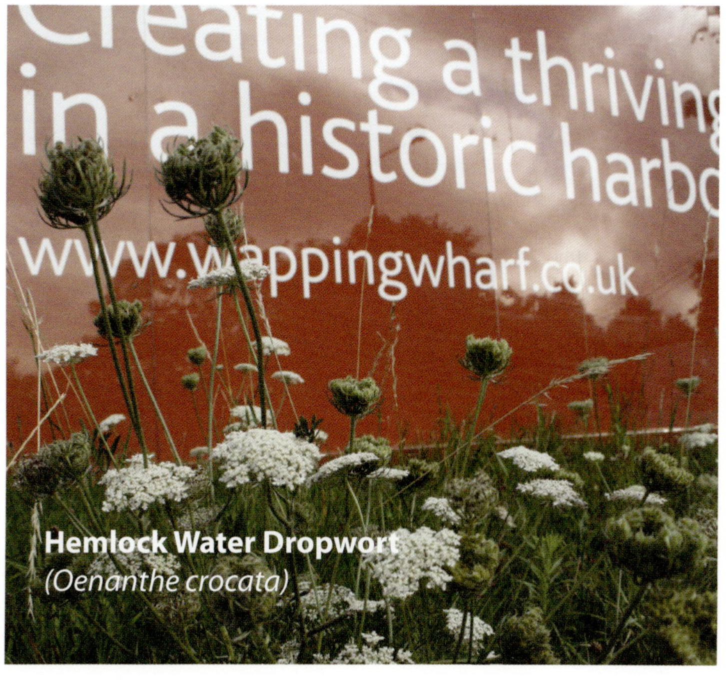

Hemlock Water Dropwort
(*Oenanthe crocata*)

Juvenile Herring Gull
(Larus argentatus)
Hovering at Bristol Docks

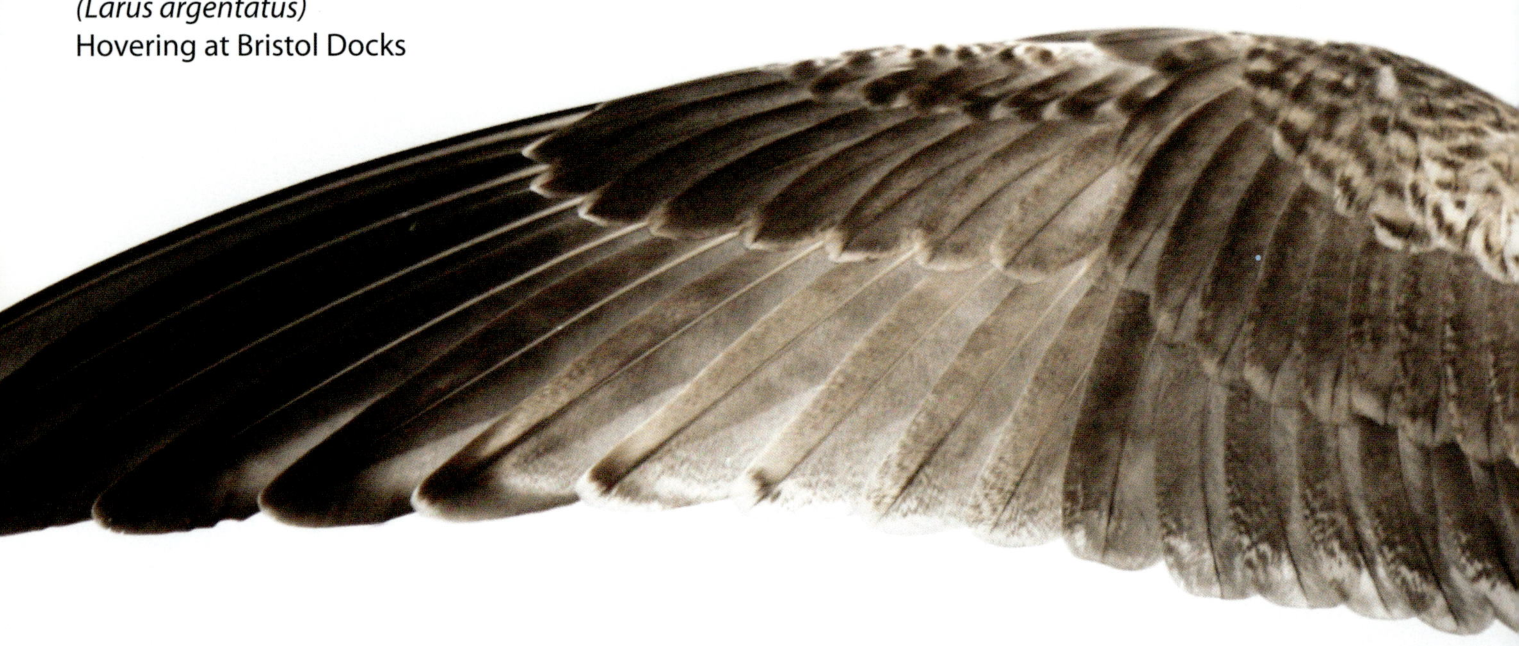

So why not head down to the harbour area and have a walk
around. Different seasons bring different plants and creatures,
and if you keep your eyes open there's always something
different to see.

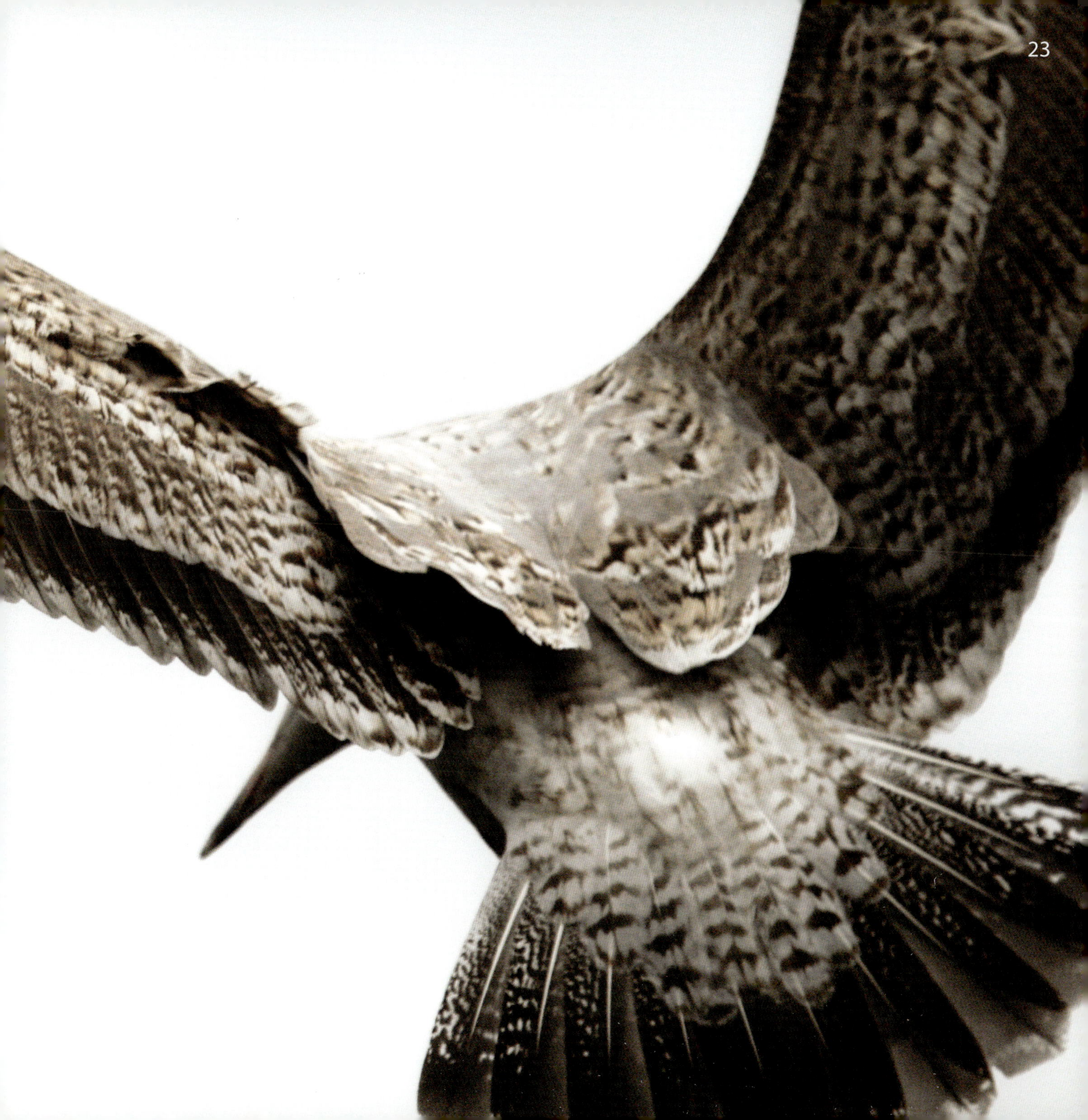

Brandon Hill
Nature Reserve

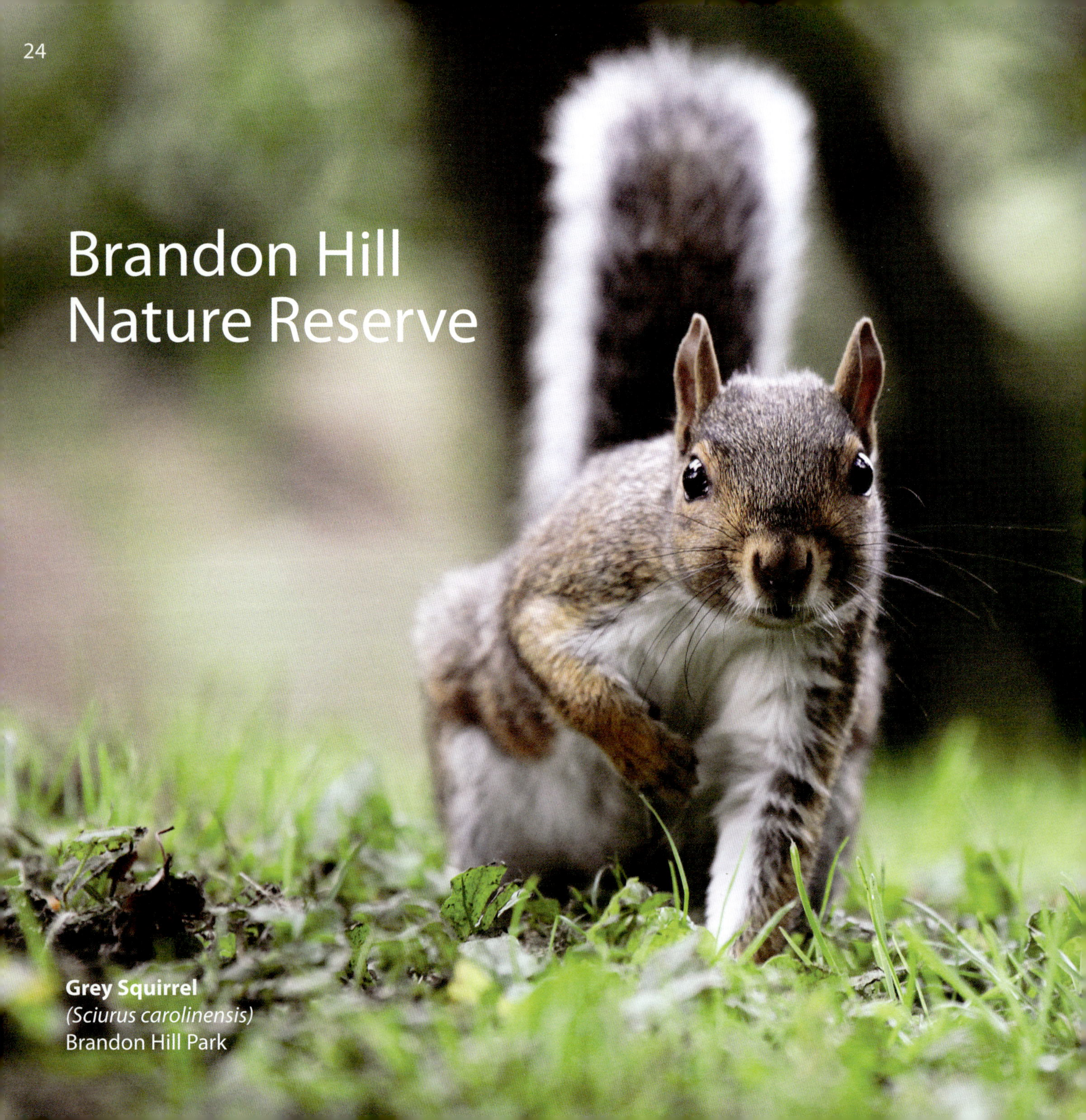

Grey Squirrel
(*Sciurus carolinensis*)
Brandon Hill Park

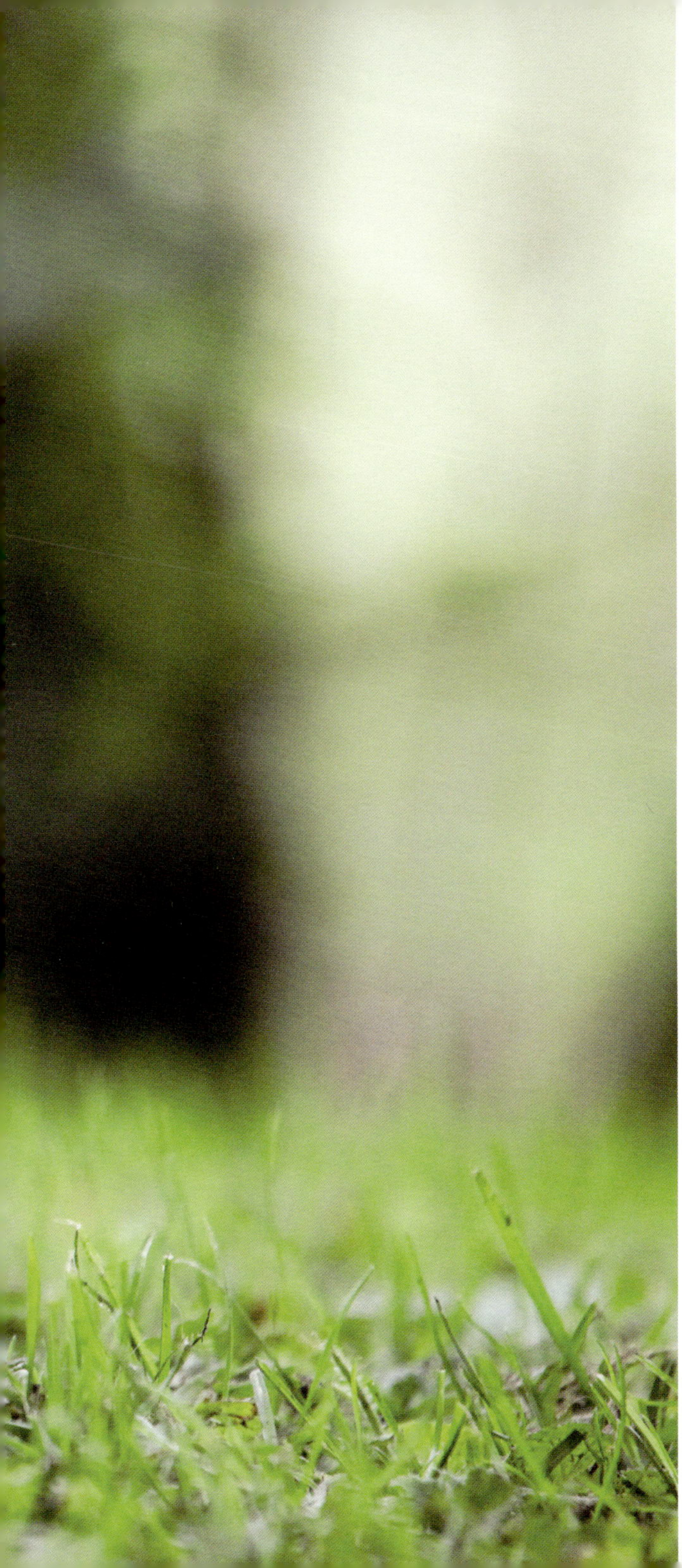

Brandon Hill Nature Reserve is managed by Avon Wildlife Trust and is my favourite green area in the whole of Bristol. The wildlife is truly astonishing and what makes this place so special is its location smack bang in the centre of the city. According to the city council's website, Brandon Hill may be the oldest municipal open space in the country, having come into the possession of Bristol Corporation in 1174. Part is set aside as a nature park and was the first of its kind in Britain.

One of the first animals to greet you will be one of the many cheeky grey squirrels busily going about their business of burying nuts. They are great ambassadors for planting trees; many of the seeds or nuts they plant as food to keep them going through the tougher winter months they simply forget and the seeds will grow into saplings and finally trees. Squirrels help keep our parks and green areas full of trees.

Now very tame, squirrels offer great opportunities for great photographs.

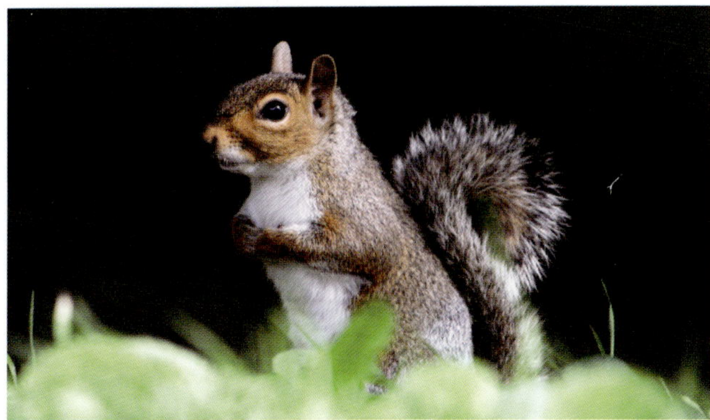

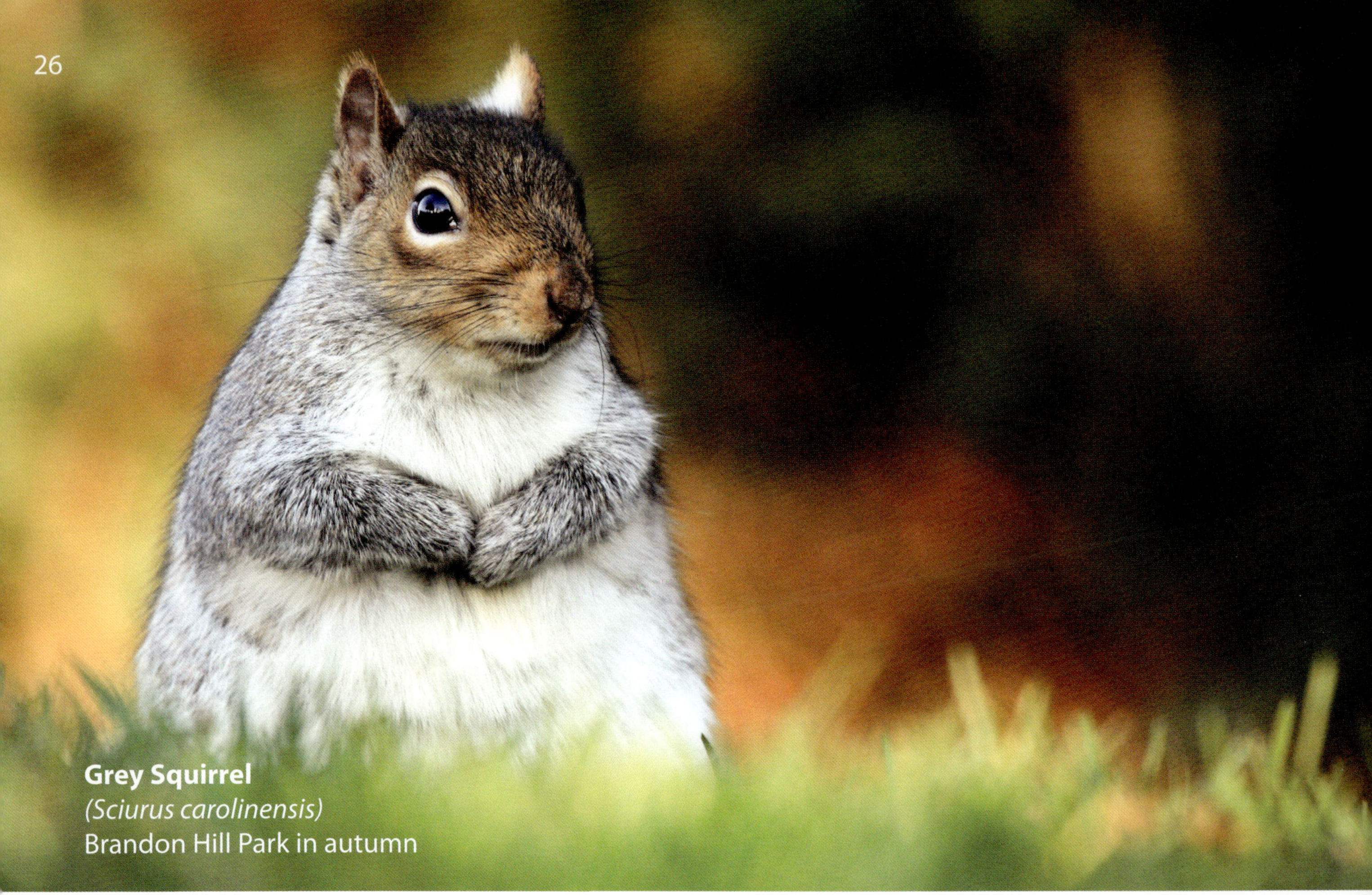

Grey Squirrel
(Sciurus carolinensis)
Brandon Hill Park in autumn

A grey squirrel's diet consists mainly of nuts, seeds and berries, all of which are plentiful on Brandon Hill. Late autumn is a good time to watch this little animal desperately burying nuts for the hard winter ahead. Birds such as jay, bullfinch and blackcap may be seen and a couple of years ago I spotted some treecreepers – a small, very active bird that lives in trees. It has a long, slender, down-curved bill. It is speckled brown above and mainly white below – well worth watching out for in the woodland walk.

Brandon Hill has a large population of foxes which live off the waste bins and left-over food from Park Street's restaurants. I've heard they are particularly fond of Chinese food. Another not so popular animal frequenting the hill is the brown rat.

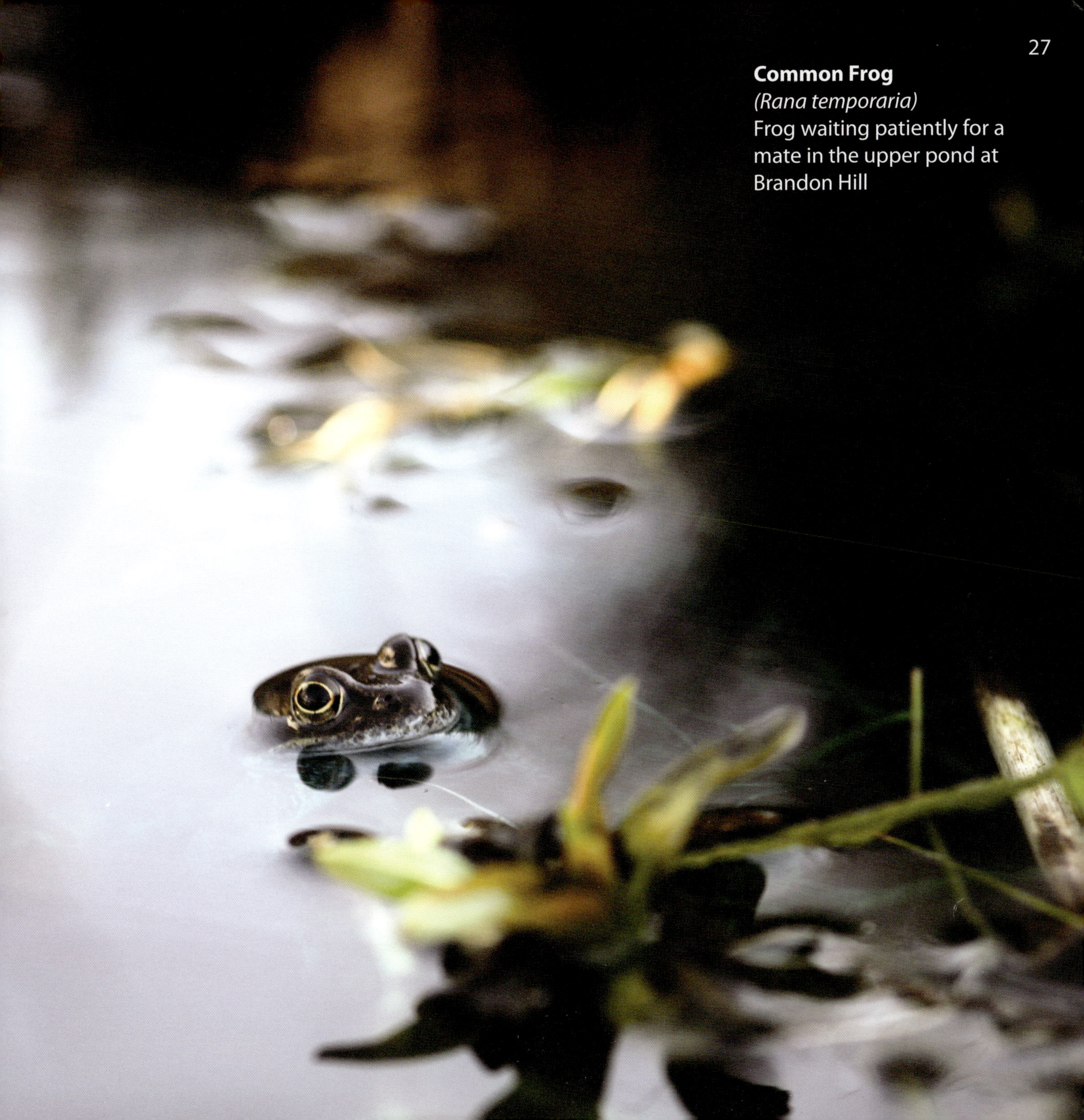

Common Frog
(Rana temporaria)
Frog waiting patiently for a
mate in the upper pond at
Brandon Hill

The upper pond near Cabot Tower in spring is a great place to watch frogs and toads spawn. The frog spawn is in clusters, and toad spawn is in thin chains. The pond is a hive of activity for three or four days at the end of February and beginning of March as the weather starts to warm up. The male frog attracts the female by croaking. I have only heard this once at Brandon hill in early spring. After spawning, most frogs return to dry land and revisit the pond later in the summer, either to bask in the shade around the pond, or cool off in the water. By late summer they'll have gone again. Some will hibernate in dry stone walls, under stones etc., whilst others will stay at the bottom of a pond in an attempt to be the first to attract females the following spring. It takes a frog three years to reach sexual maturity and it usually returns to its home pond to spawn.

Smooth newt, also known as the common newt, has made its home in the pond here. Adult smooth newts emerge from hibernation on land from February and head to fresh water to breed. They favour ponds and shallow lakesides over running water. Brandon Hill is a perfect environment for them.

There are three-spined sticklebacks in great numbers in this pond. Sticklebacks have various forms of life cycle. Some stay in freshwater all the time, as in this pond, while others behave more like salmon and migrate to the sea for their adult lives returning to freshwater to breed. In the far north of England, for example, sticklebacks migrate, spending winter in the sea and returning to fresh water in the spring.

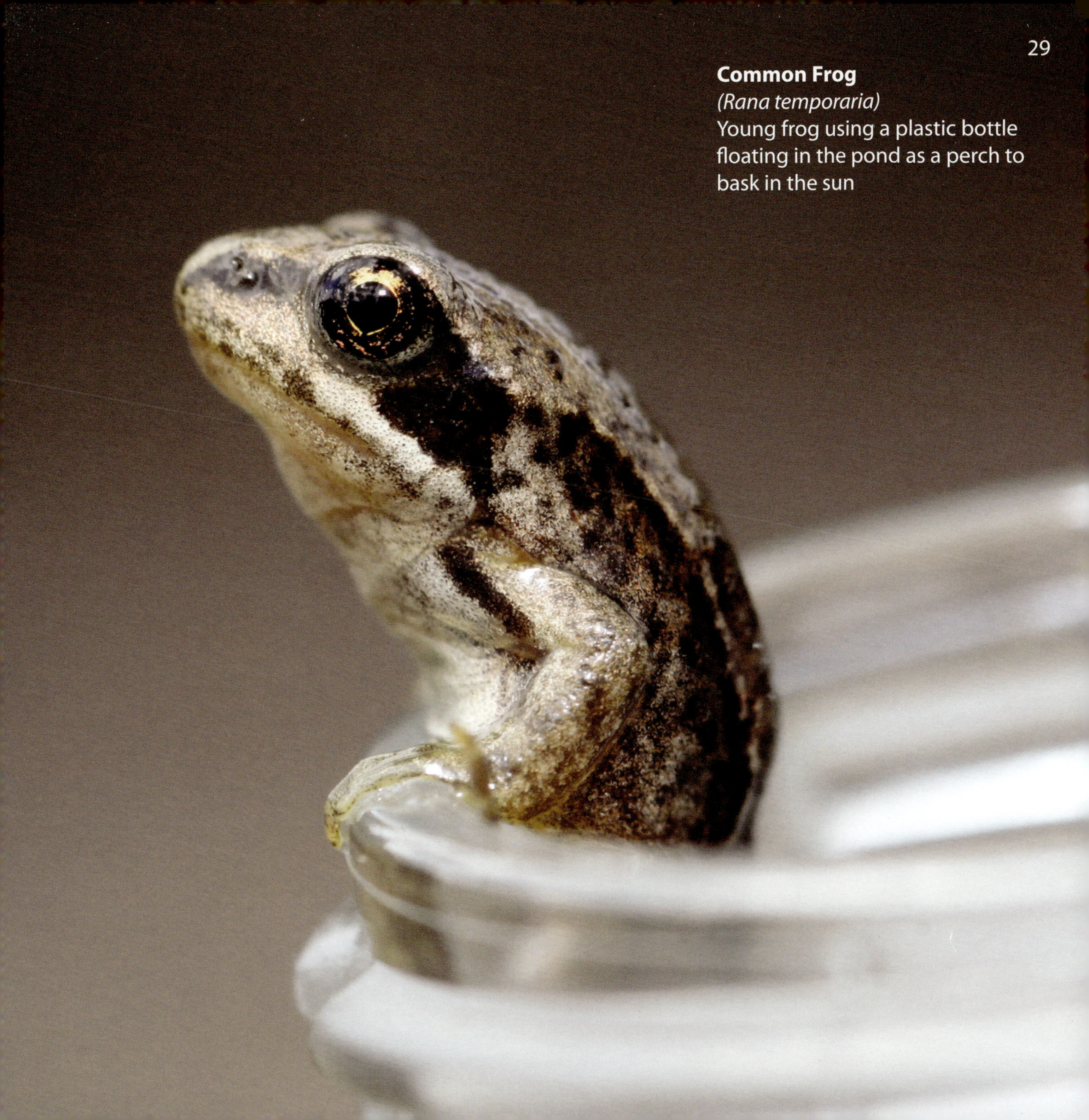

Common Frog
(Rana temporaria)
Young frog using a plastic bottle floating in the pond as a perch to bask in the sun

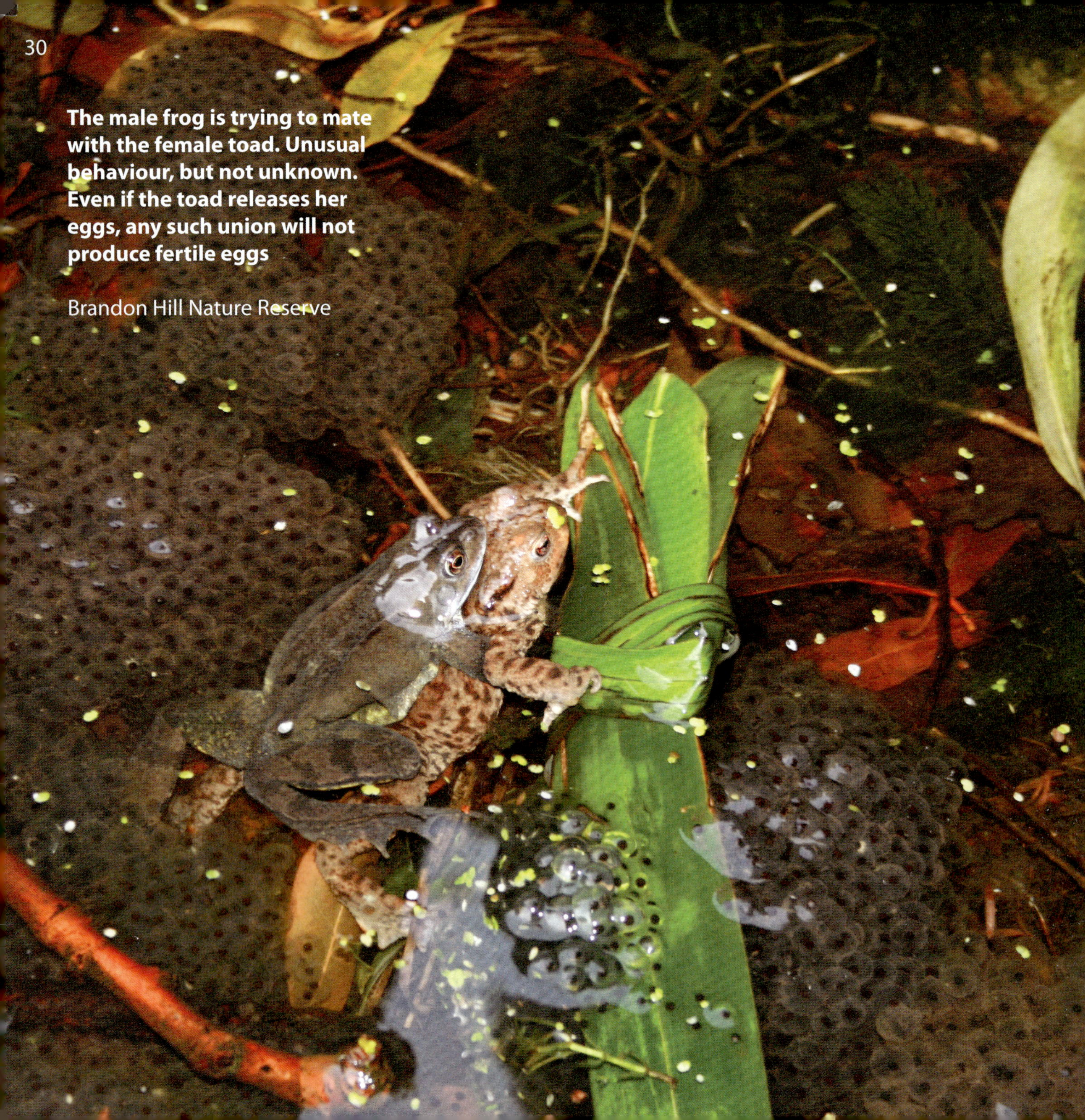

The male frog is trying to mate with the female toad. Unusual behaviour, but not unknown. Even if the toad releases her eggs, any such union will not produce fertile eggs

Brandon Hill Nature Reserve

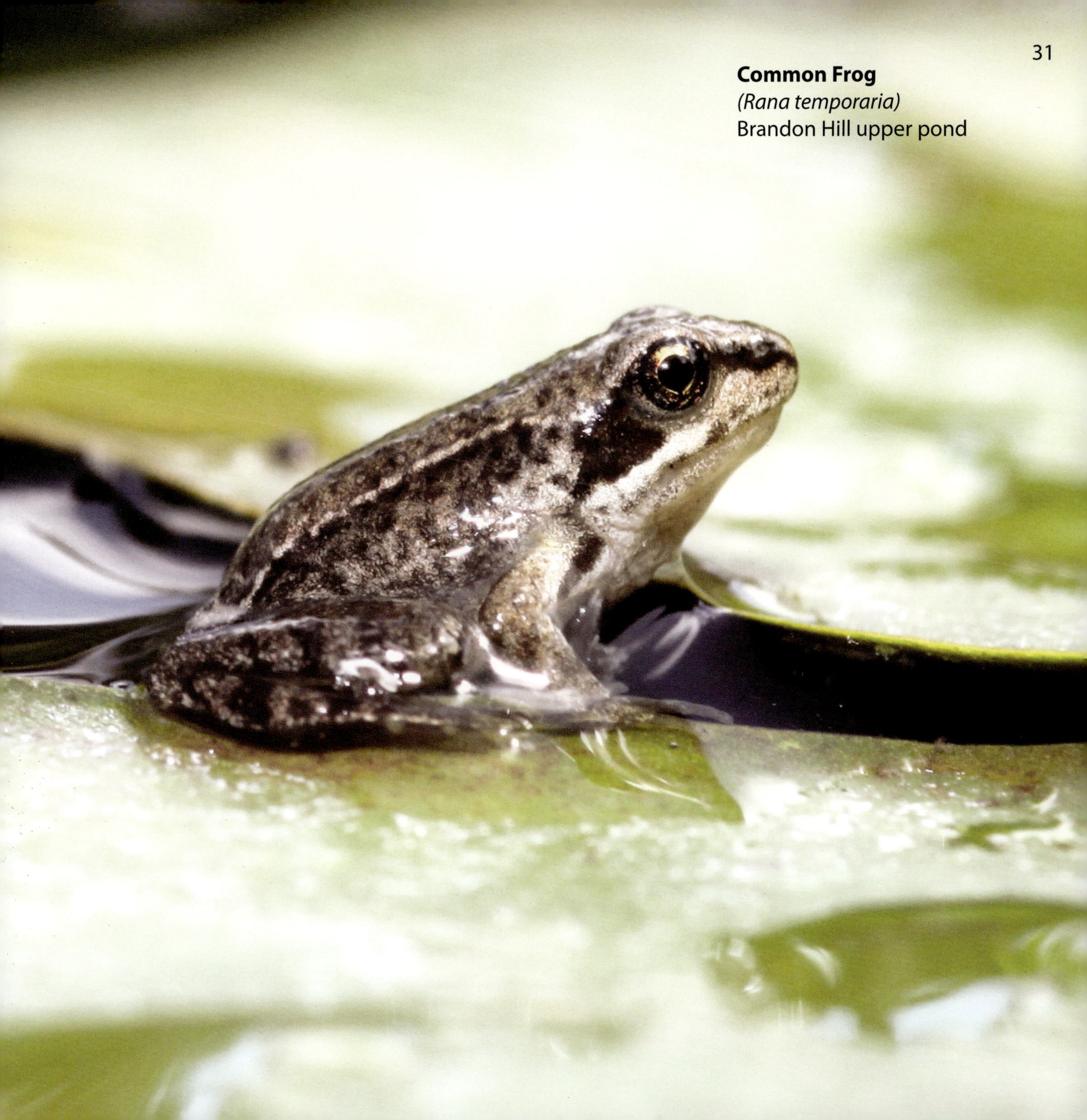

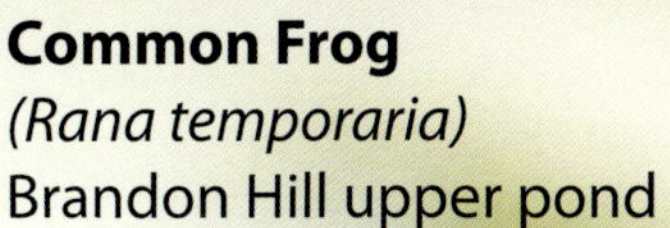

Common Frog
(Rana temporaria)
Brandon Hill upper pond

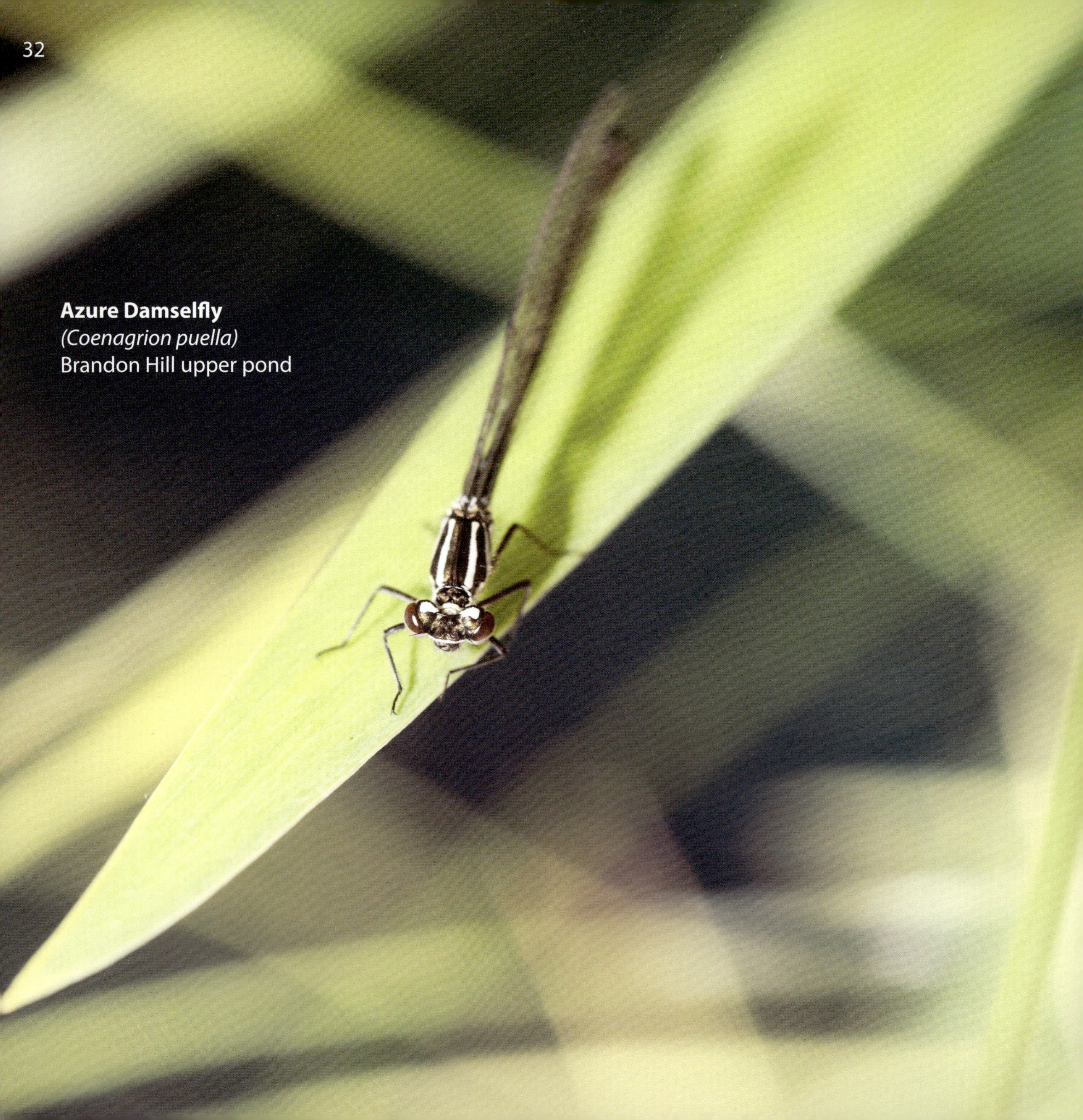

Azure Damselfly
(Coenagrion puella)
Brandon Hill upper pond

The upper and lower ponds on Brandon Hill are great places to see damselflies. Most have a life cycle of one year but some species take two years. The adults mate over the shallow water, either in flight, or when clinging on to the exposed parts of water plants. After mating, the female crawls into the water to lay her eggs on the submerged portion of the vegetation. The larva or nymph soon hatches, feeding on small water creatures.

It heads to the deeper water of the pond in the autumn to hibernate, returning to the shallow water the following spring, when it will crawl up a stem of a water plant and turn into a beautiful damselfly, starting the life cycle all over again.

Conops Fly
(Conops quadrifasciatus)
Resting on a leaf in the summer
meadow at Brandon Hill

The wildflower meadow is at its
best in midsummer, when ox-eye
daisies, yellow rattle and knapweed
add a pleasant burst of colour.
Insects include flies, butterflies and
crickets. The conops fly is pictured
above. Fertilized females lay their
eggs in flight, on slow-flying hosts
(bees, bumble bees or wasps).
The larvae hatch and burrow into
the abdomen of their host and
feed on their insides until they are
empty shells.

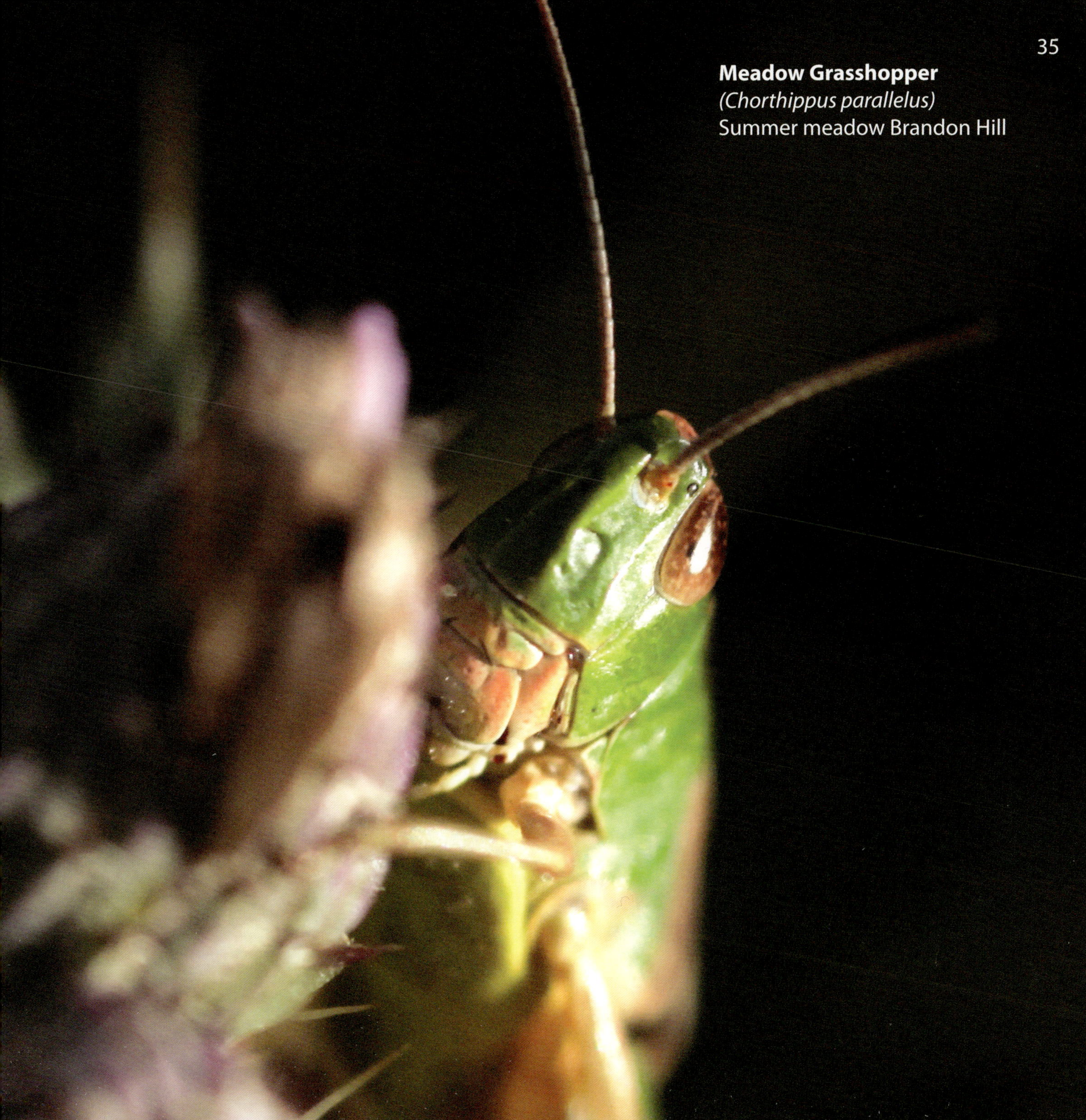

Meadow Grasshopper
(Chorthippus parallelus)
Summer meadow Brandon Hill

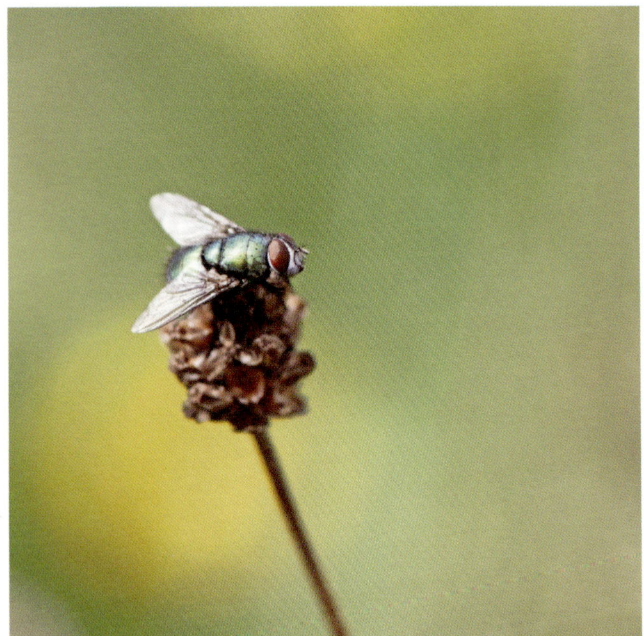

Common Green Bottle Fly
(Lucilia sericata)

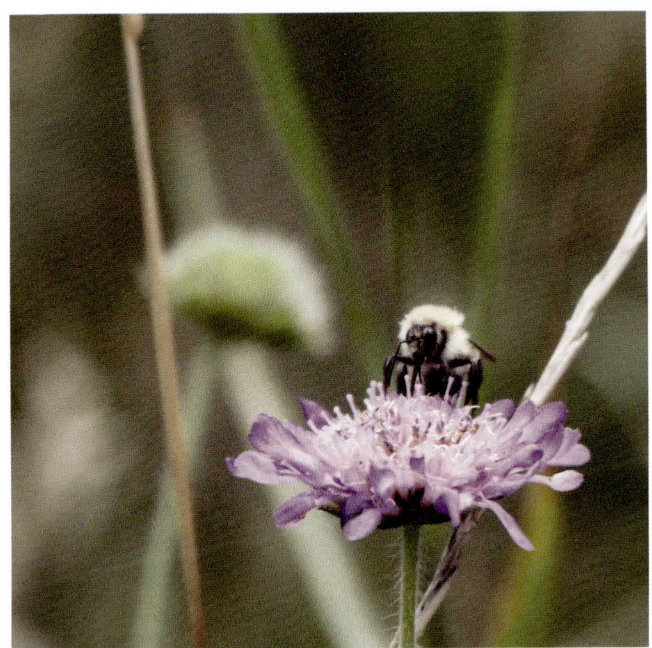

Buff-tailed Bumble Bee
(Bombus terrestris)

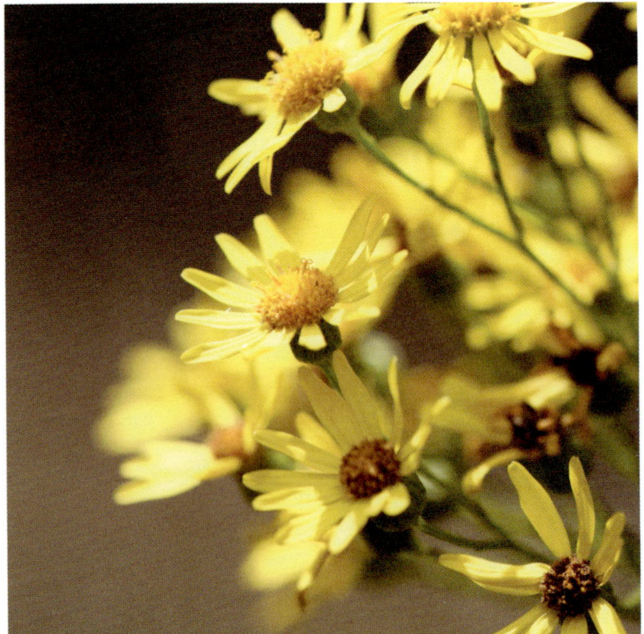

Ragwort
(Senecio jacobaea)

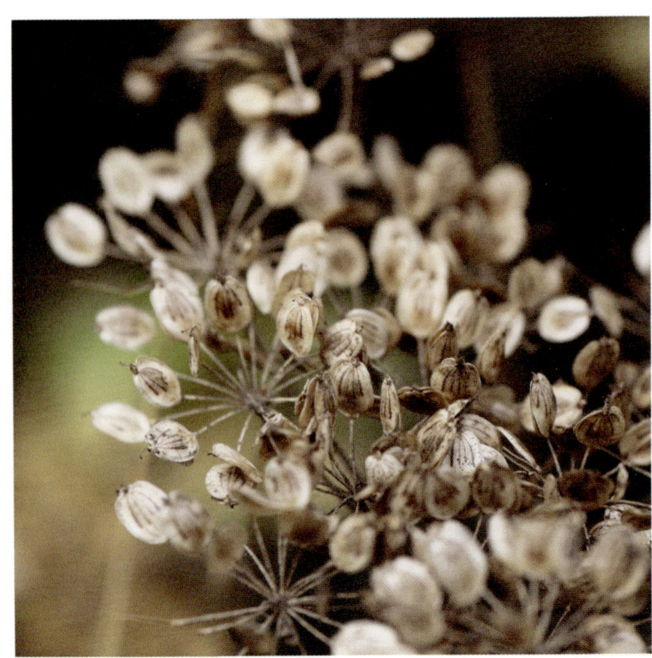

Common Hogweed
(Heracleum sphondylium)

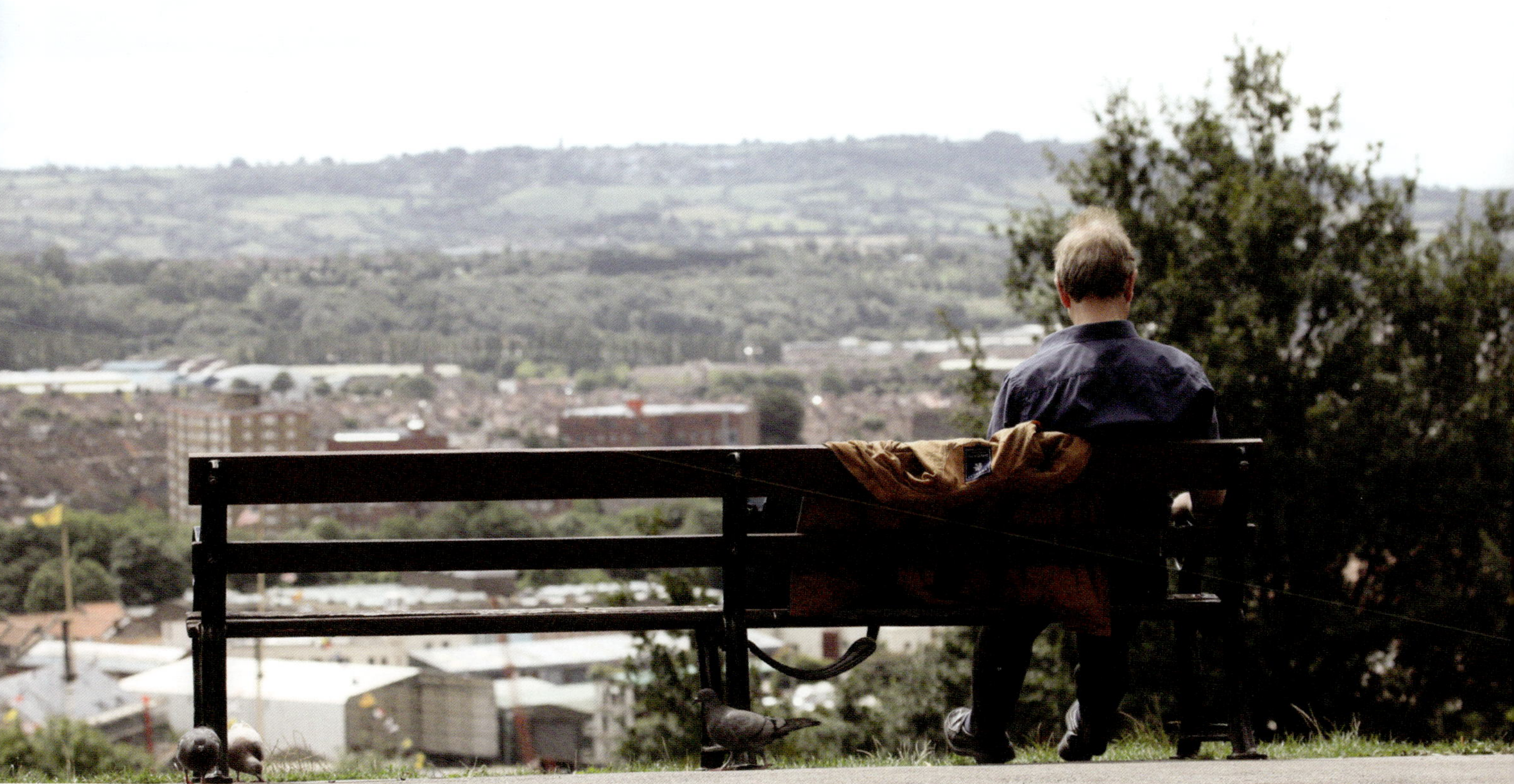

View from Brandon Hill across
the river

I always think a welcome sound of the summer is the bumble bee collecting the nectar and pollen from the many different flowers in the meadow. The bee stops from time to time to gently brush the pollen off its hairy body into tiny pollen baskets which are found on its hind legs.

Another colourful insect everyone has a soft spot for is the ladybird and this park during the summer months attracts its fair share. European folk lore has it that ladybirds bring good luck because they are messengers to heaven. There are 46 species in Britain but the most likely for you to see are the two-spot and seven-spot ladybirds. As the winter draws closer keep a look out in your homes and sheds as these insects look for dry and warm places to spend the colder months.

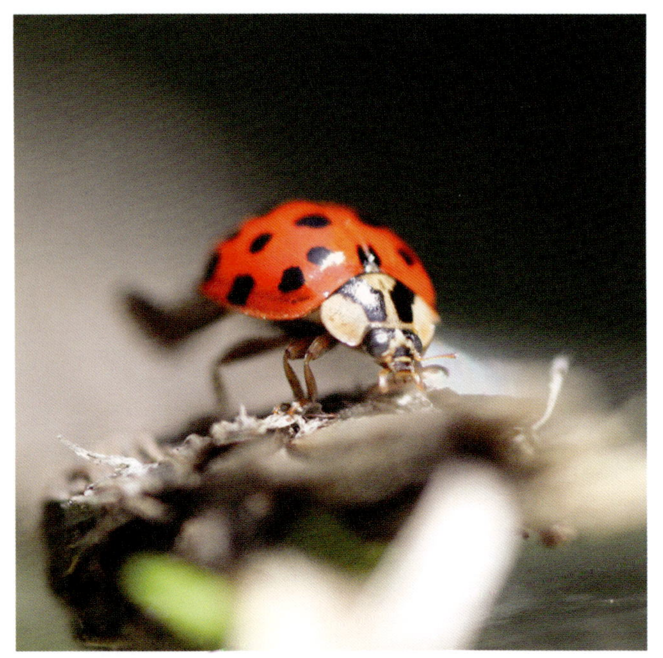
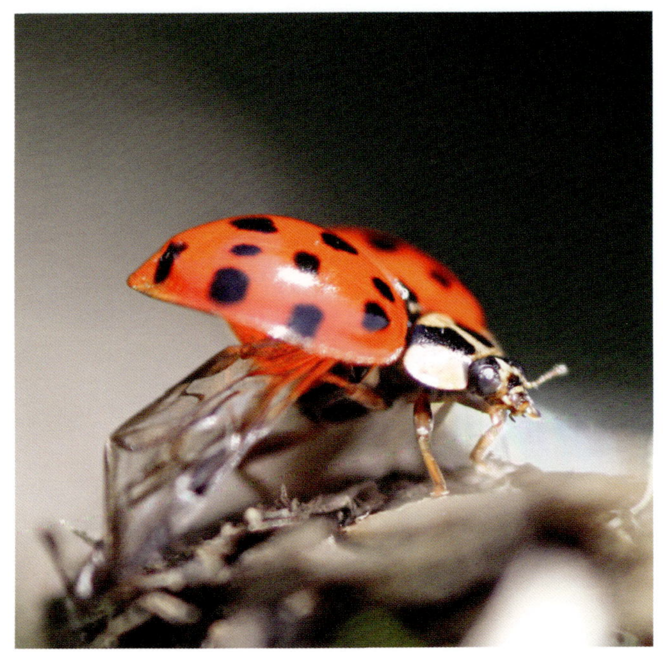
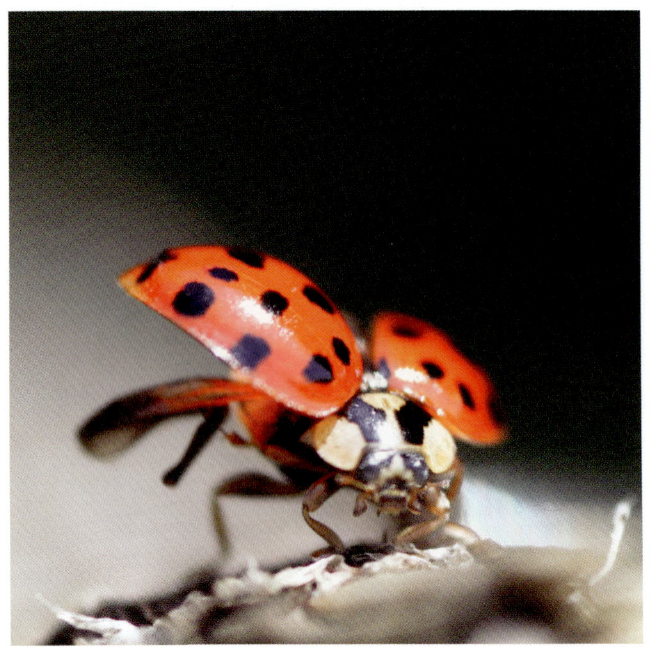
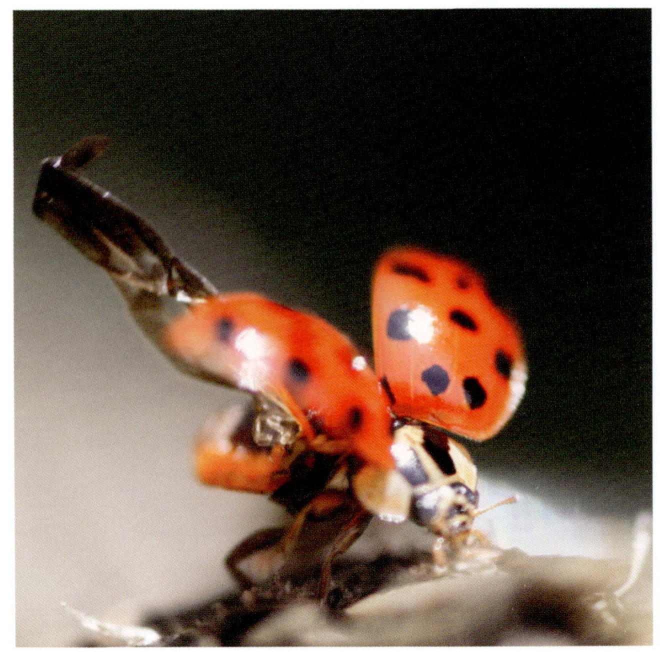

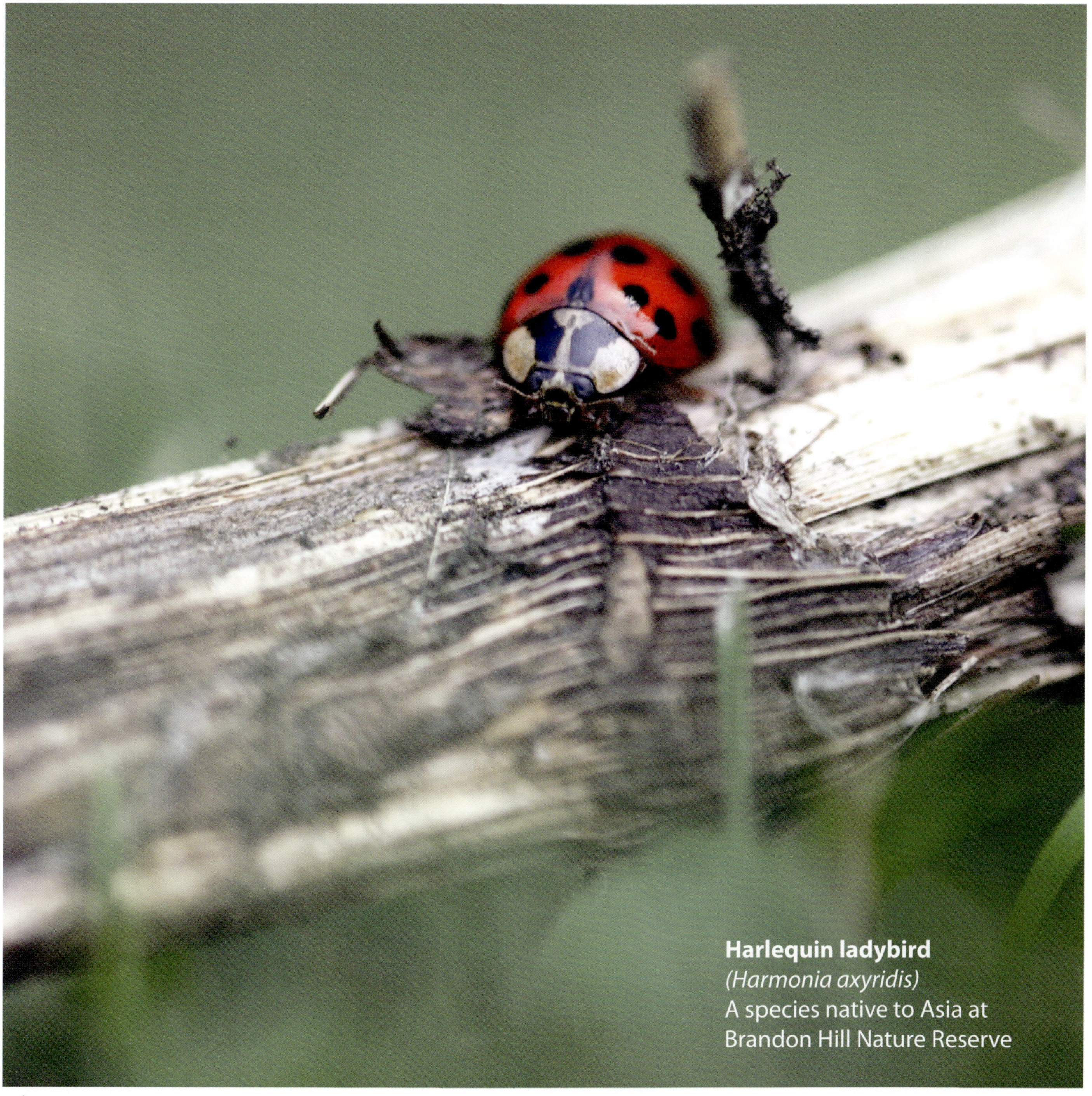

Harlequin ladybird
(Harmonia axyridis)
A species native to Asia at
Brandon Hill Nature Reserve

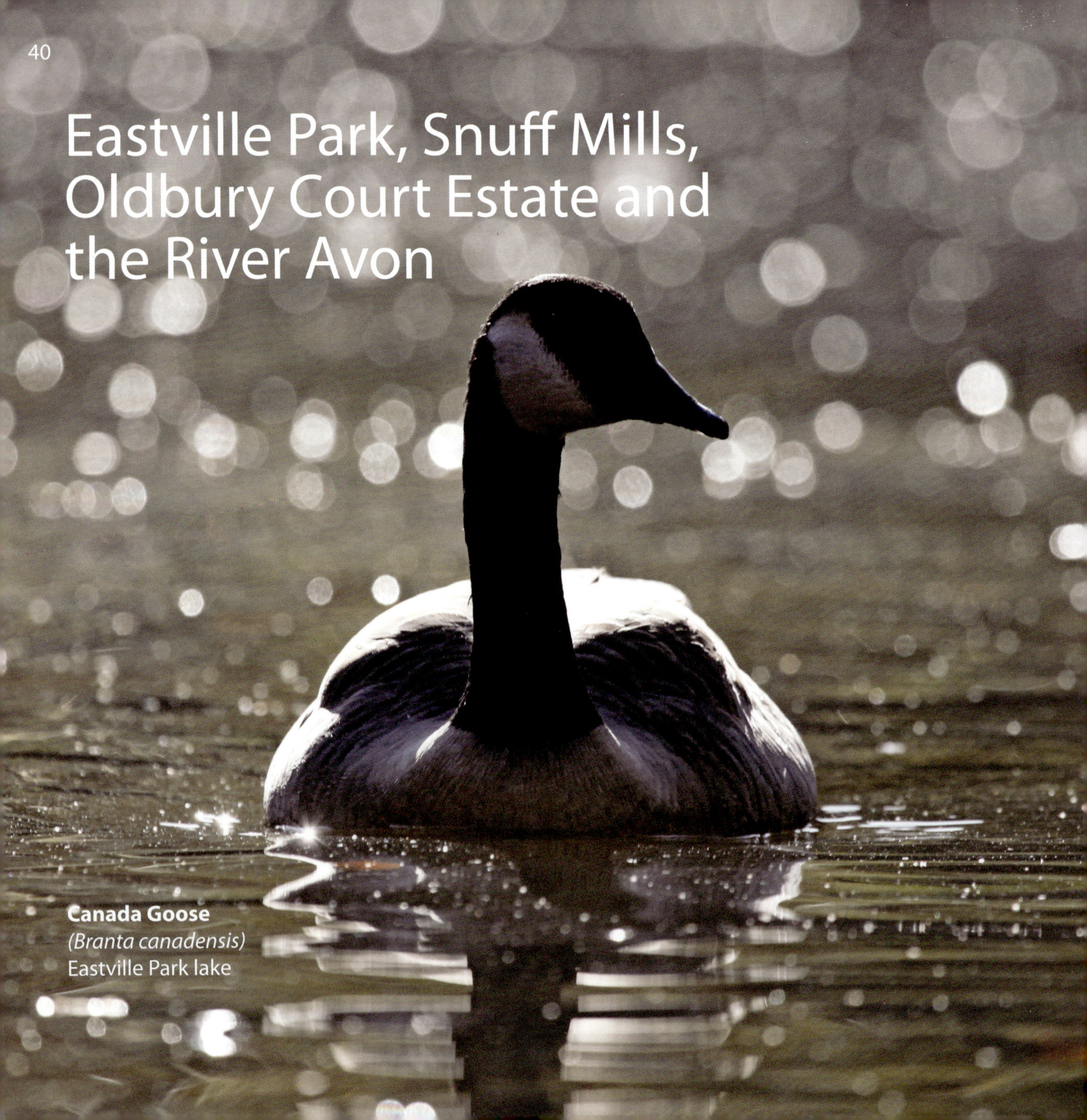

Eastville Park, Snuff Mills, Oldbury Court Estate and the River Avon

Canada Goose
(Branta canadensis)
Eastville Park lake

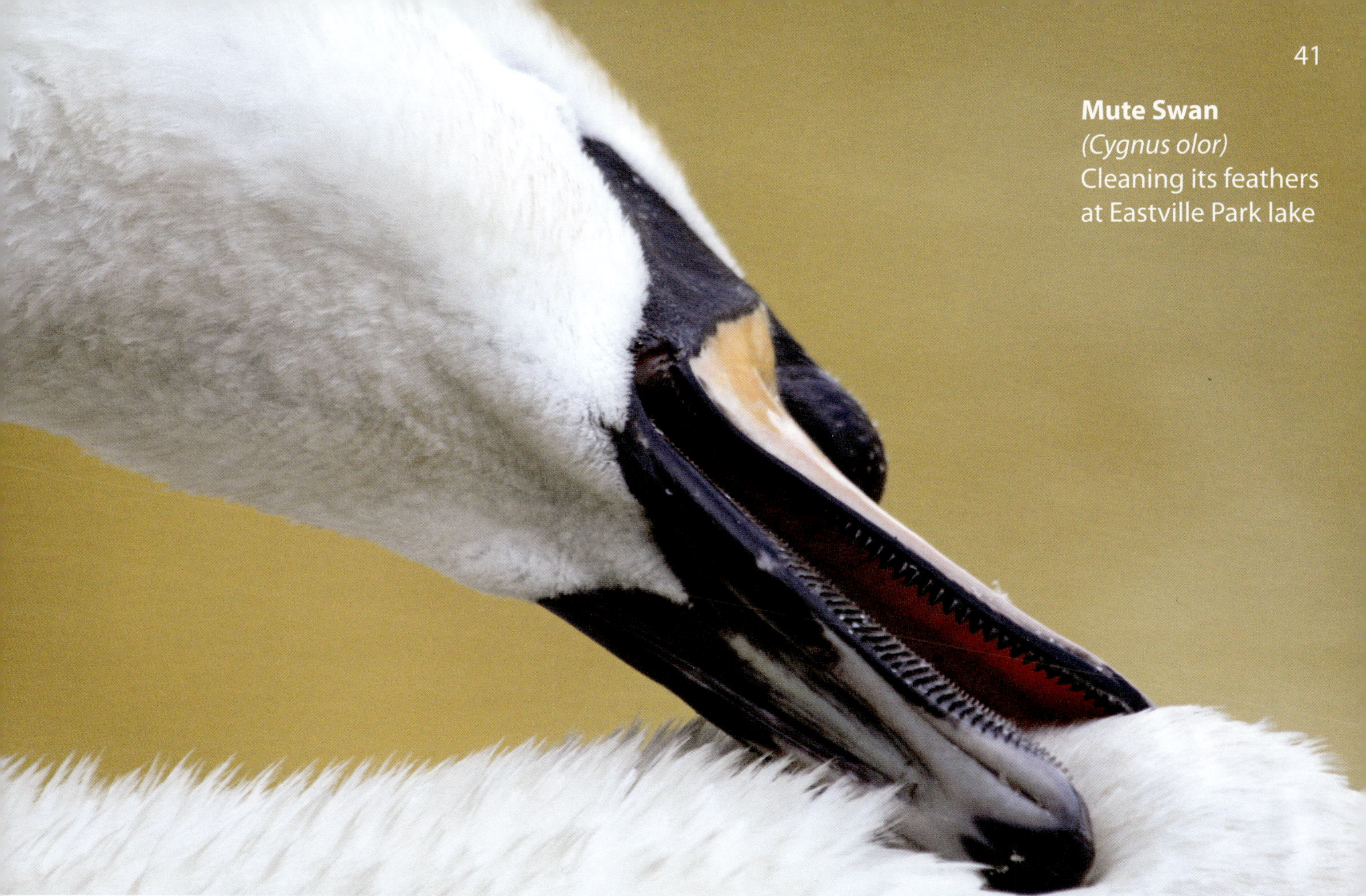

This is an important area for wildlife. It is a green corridor which allows people to see a vast array of creatures from elusive kingfishers, otters and tawny owls to the more common mute swans and coots right in the centre of Bristol. This is a special area; at times it feels as if you are in the countryside and miles from the city. At places the high valley walls block out the sound of traffic and other urban noise.

Eastville Park ornamental lake is a good place to see water birds: ducks, swans, Canada geese and the occasional grey heron patiently waiting for a fish. Spring time cygnets swim closely behind their parents copying and learning from their every move. The mute swan was given Royal status in the twelfth century, and to steal a swan's egg was punishable by imprisonment for a year and one day.

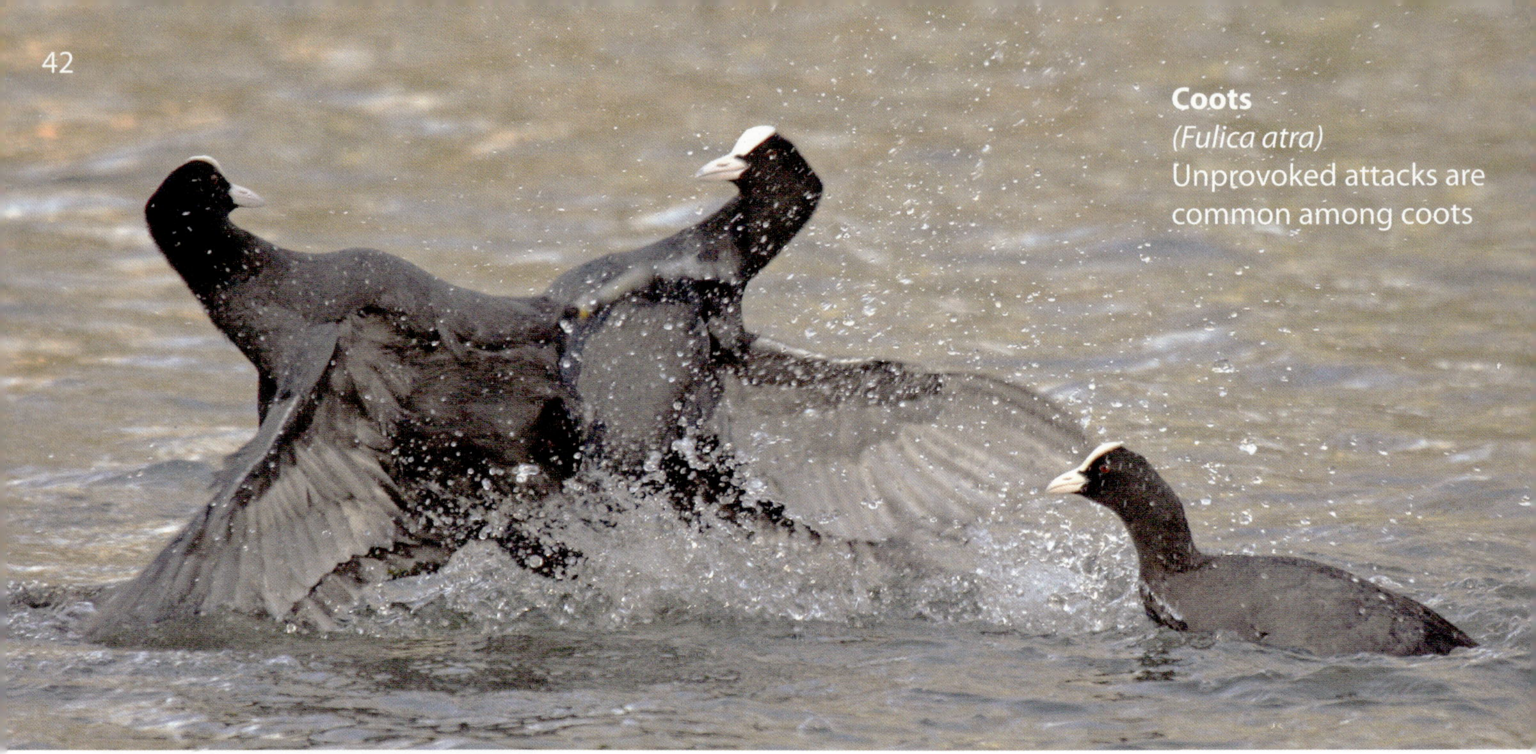

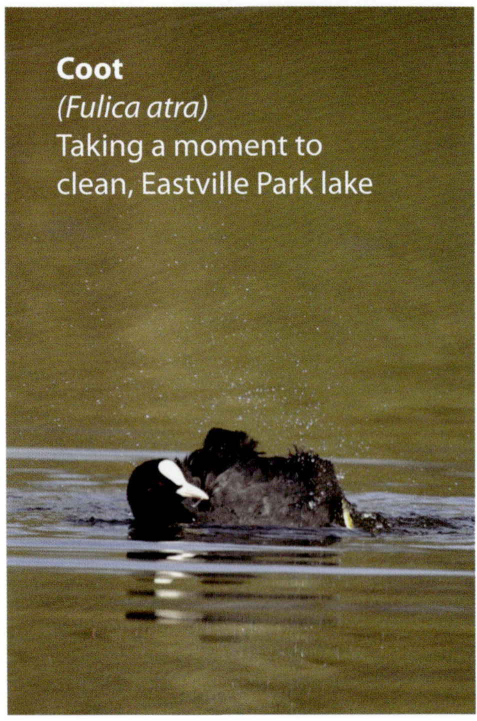

Coot
(Fulica atra)
Taking a moment to
clean, Eastville Park lake

A bird you will always see here is the coot – an energetic but often clumsy diver, submerging for a few seconds then bobbing back up, often tail first. Many times here I've seen coots fighting. Coots and moorhens share this water and are sometimes confused but are easily differentiated by the colour of their bill and forehead. Coots have a white beak and forehead whilst moorhens have a bright red bill, with a yellow tip.

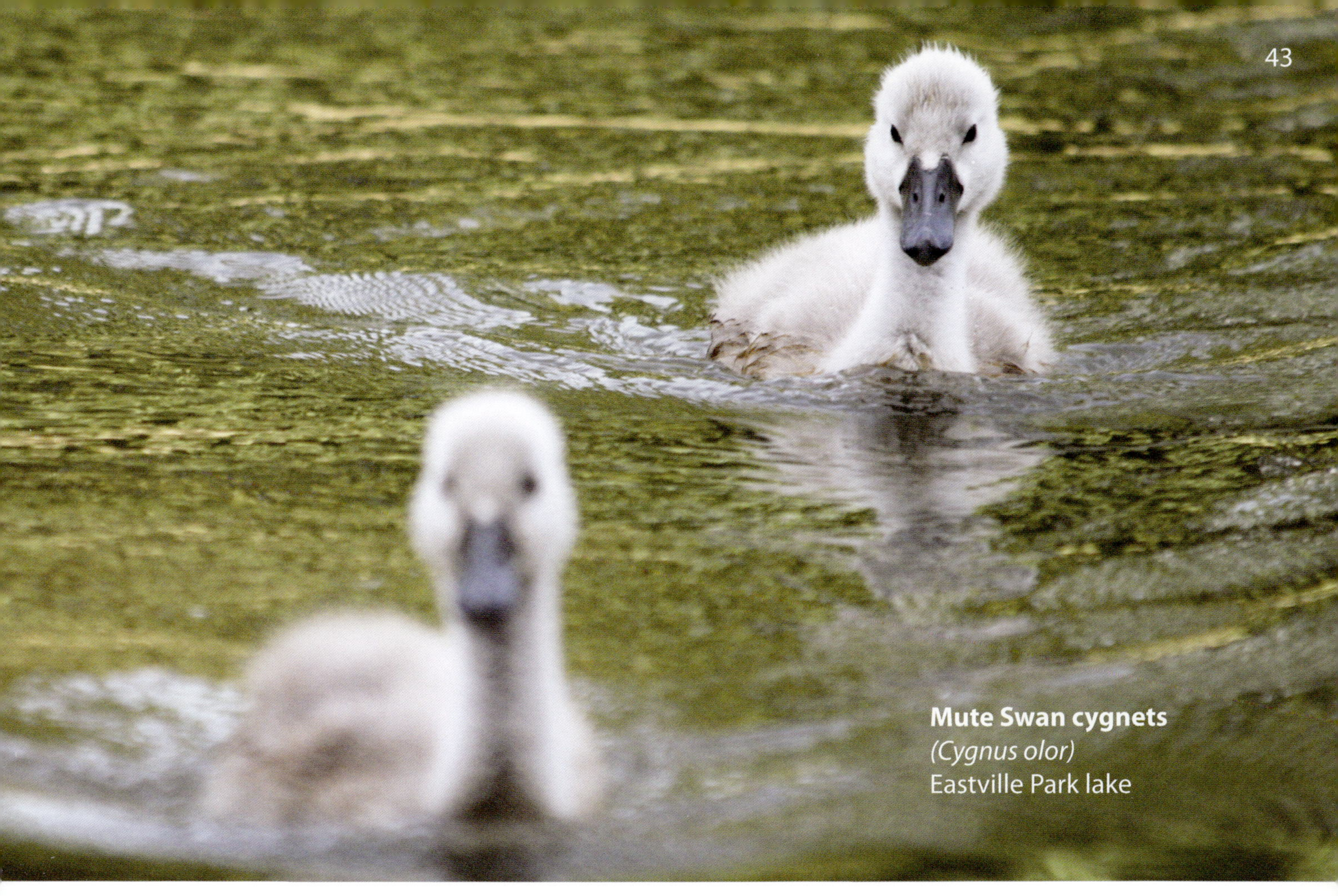

Mute Swan cygnets
(Cygnus olor)
Eastville Park lake

Follow the River Frome down from Eastville Park to Snuff Mills. You will find a renovated water mill, but snuff was actually milled further up the river. One of the millers was known as 'Snuffy Jack' because his smock was always covered in snuff. Wildlife which can be seen here include tawny owls, foxes, badgers, kingfishers, dippers, native crayfish and otters. That would be an impressive list for the countryside, let alone the city. Bats have made their home in the valley at Snuff Mills and at dusk take to the skies. There are common pipistrelle and Daubenton's bats, the latter also known as water bats as they feed over the river snatching small insects close to the water – a truly breathtaking display that I have witnessed at Snuff Mills with the aid of a bat detector and a flash light. Another creature feeding on insects here is the dipper, which actually walks on the river bed hunting aquatic animals. These birds nest on the rocky banks either side of the River Frome.

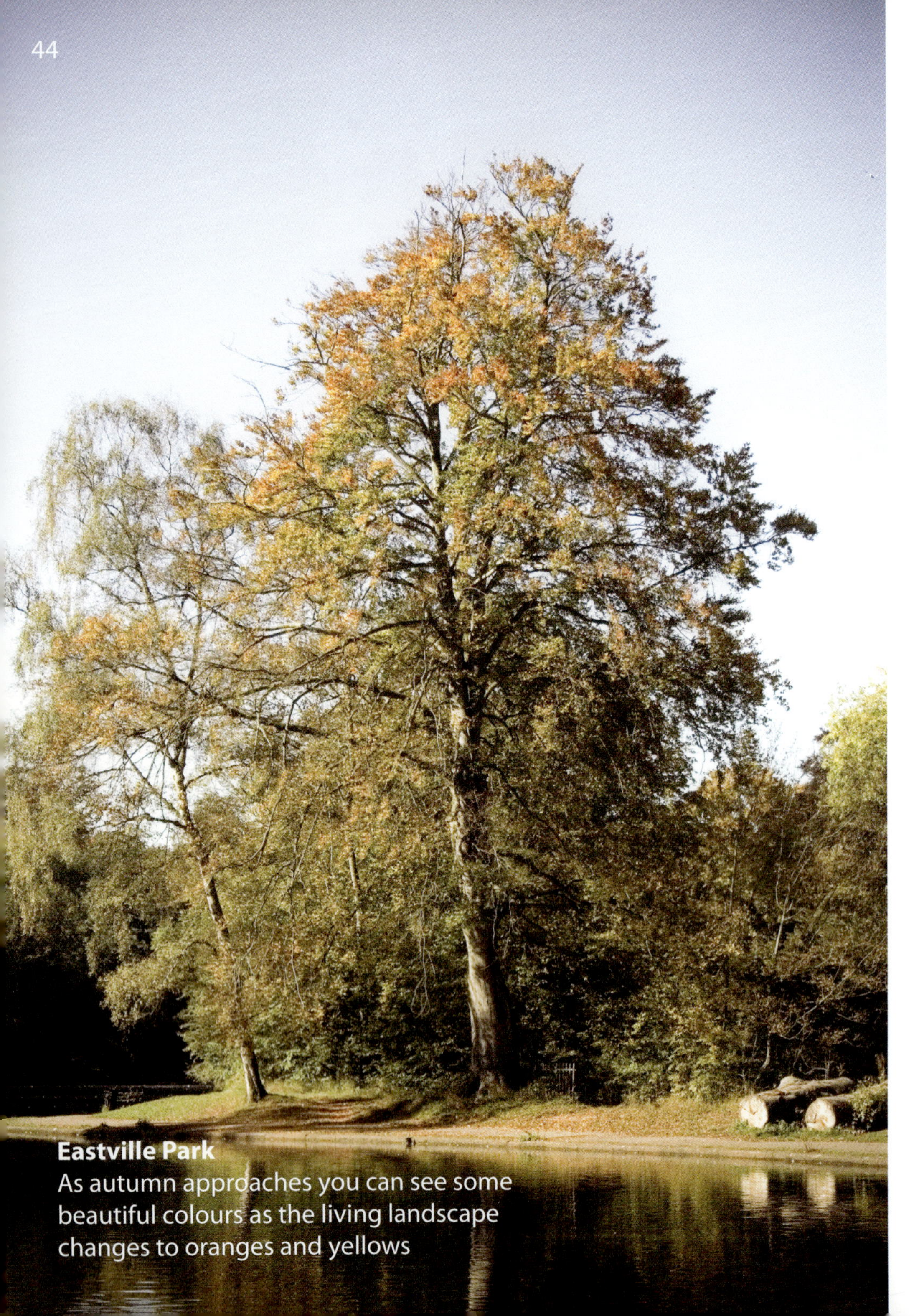

Eastville Park
As autumn approaches you can see some
beautiful colours as the living landscape
changes to oranges and yellows

Kingfishers also live on this stretch of the river. These elusive little birds are hard to see. Usually you will just catch a blue flash as the bird darts past along the river bank. The overhanging branches and riverside trees found along the river between Eastville and Winterbourne are its ideal habitat. Keep an eye out near the café at Snuff Mills car park.

One animal I would love to photograph is the otter. Experts have combed the river and found otter spraints (poo) at Snuff Mills which is conclusive evidence that otters live there. There is also a healthy collection of fish here: trout, chub, roach, perch and native crayfish. Tawny owls live in the woods near the river. Several pairs have territories along the river here and can be heard calling to each other at night.

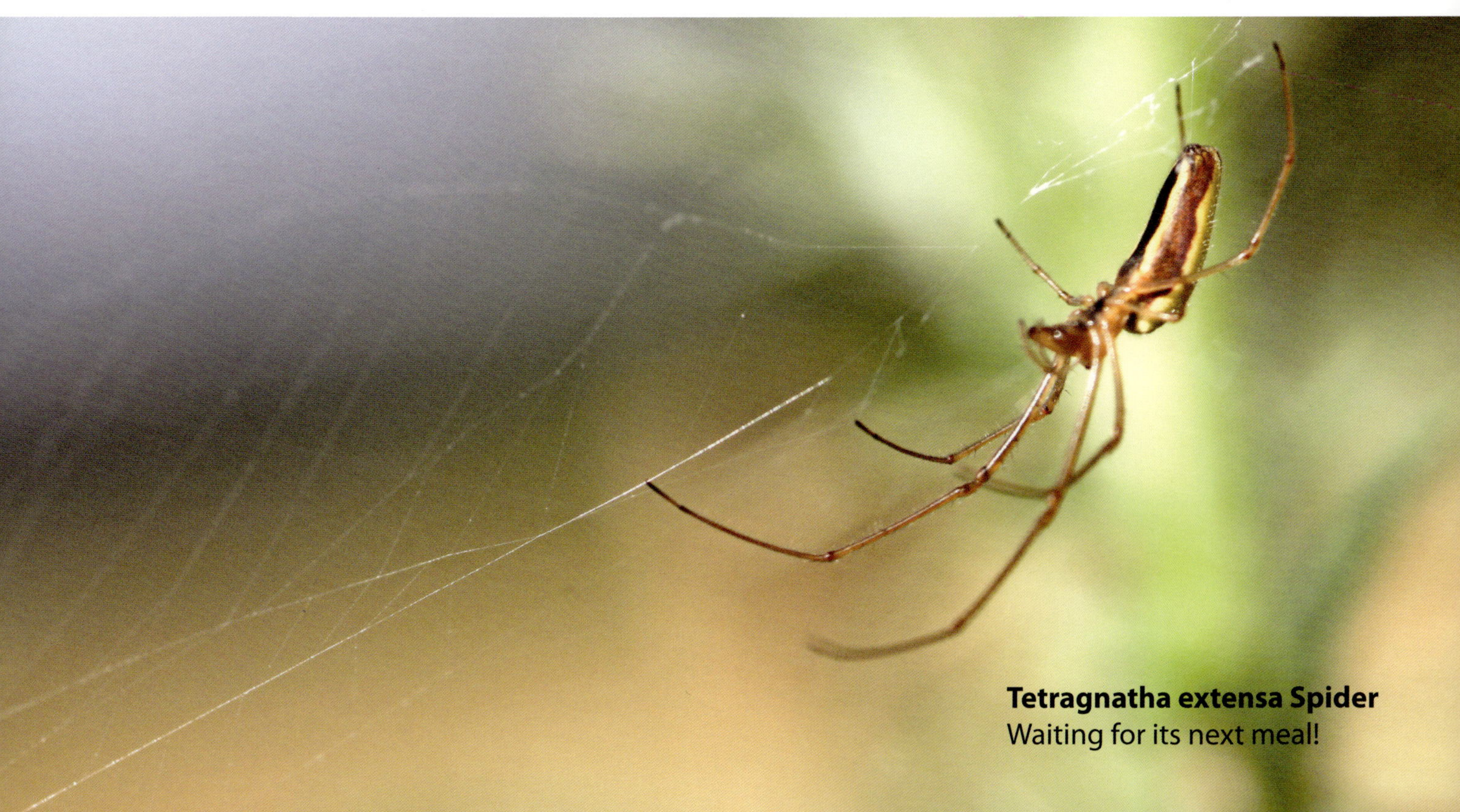

Tetragnatha extensa Spider
Waiting for its next meal!

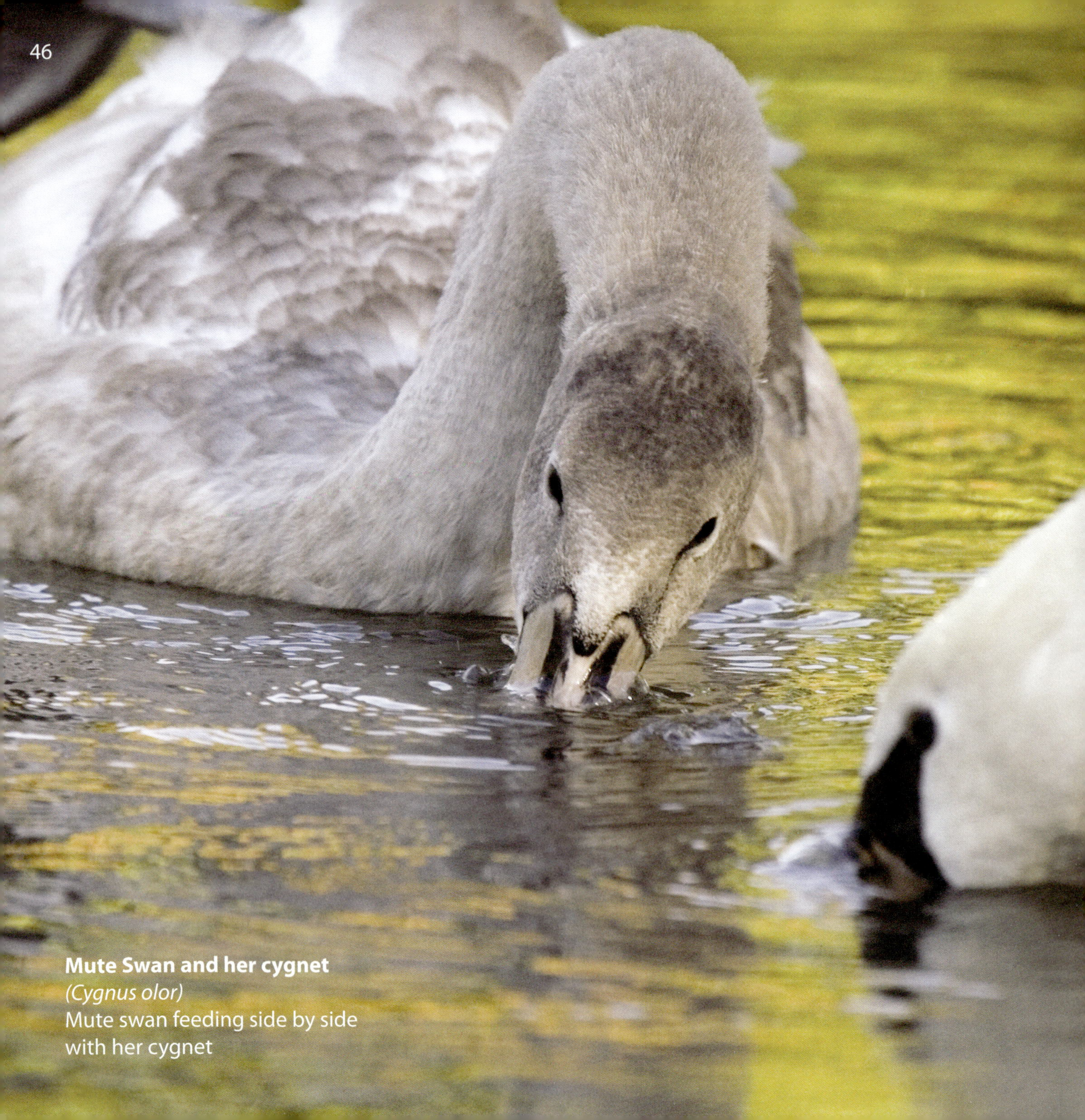

Mute Swan and her cygnet
(Cygnus olor)
Mute swan feeding side by side
with her cygnet

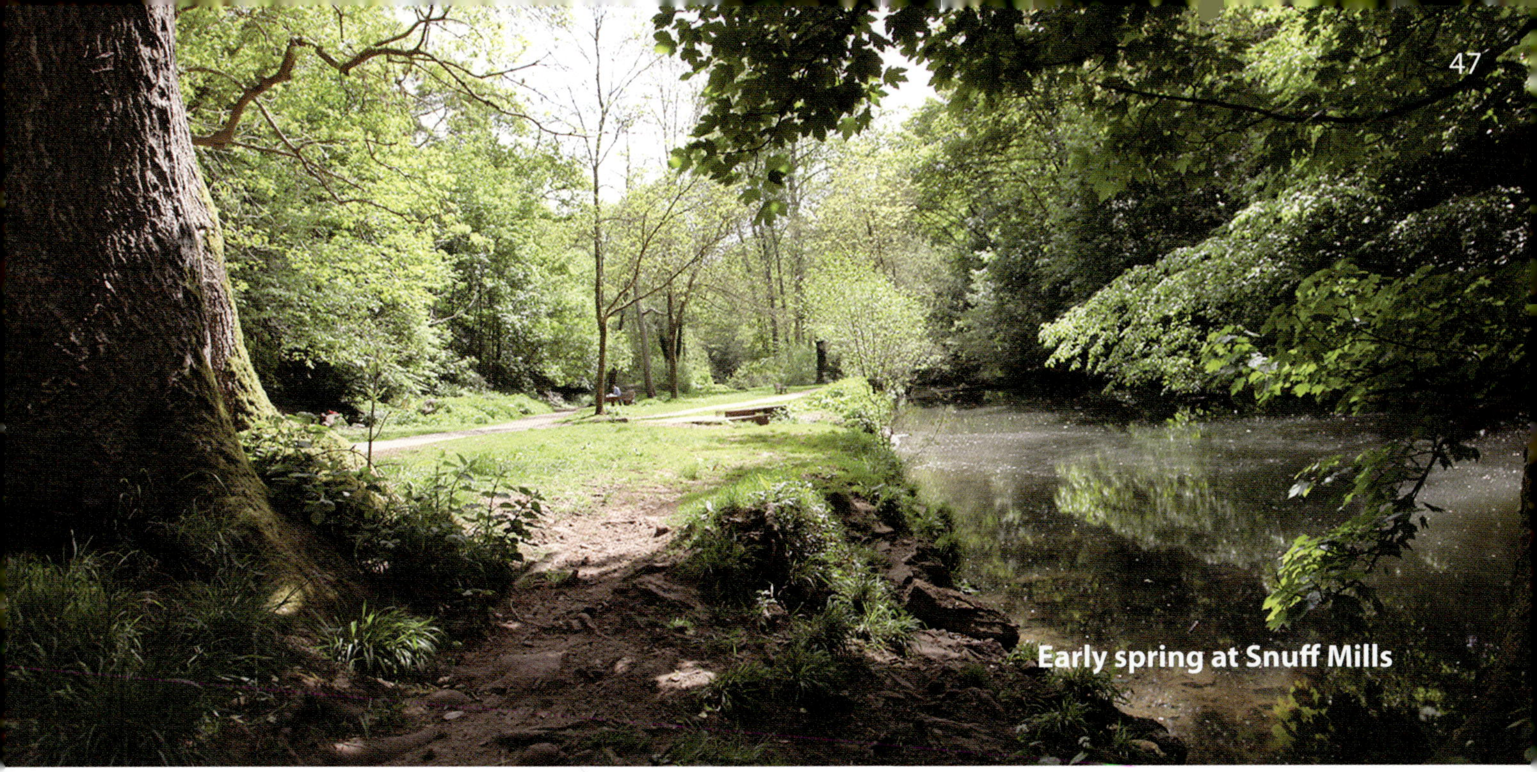

Early spring at Snuff Mills

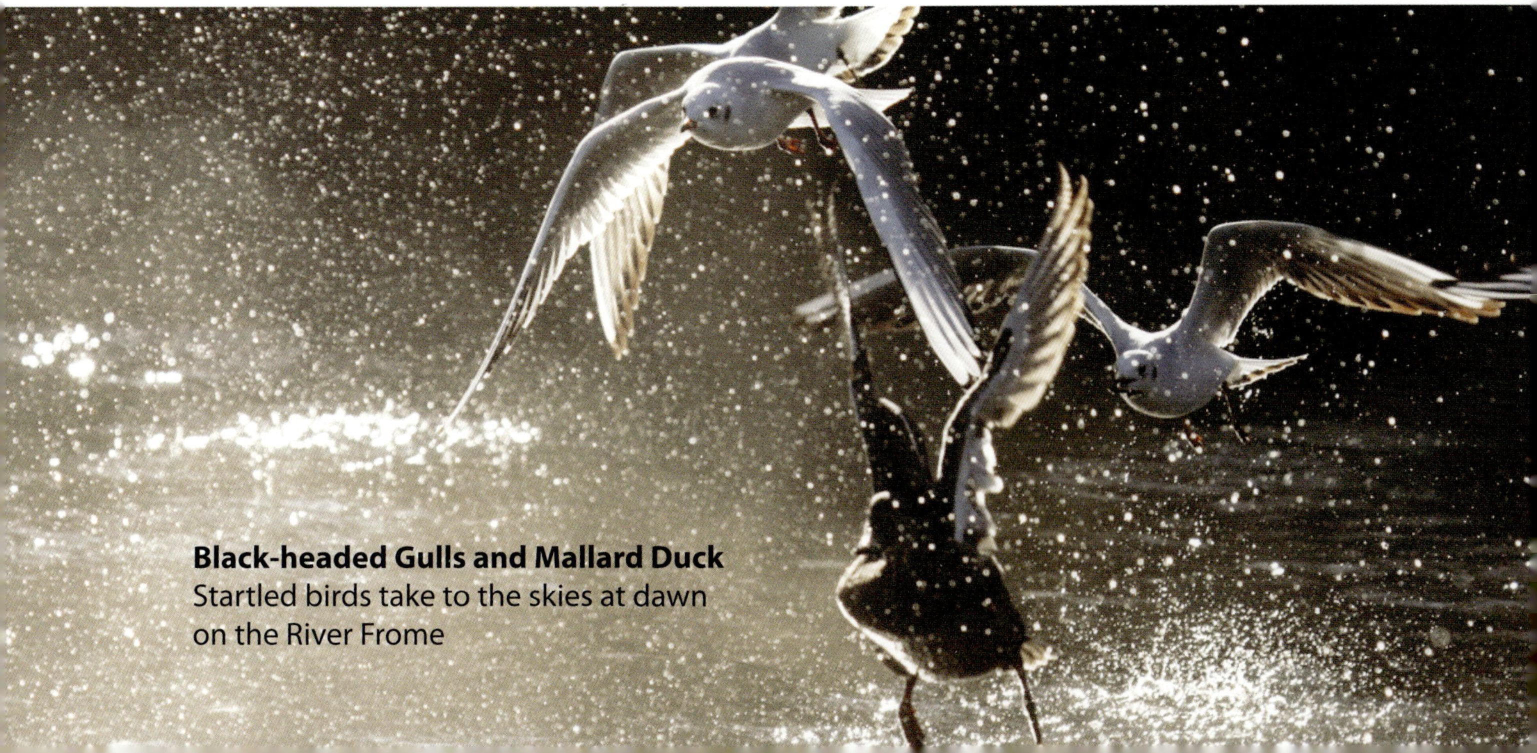

Black-headed Gulls and Mallard Duck
Startled birds take to the skies at dawn
on the River Frome

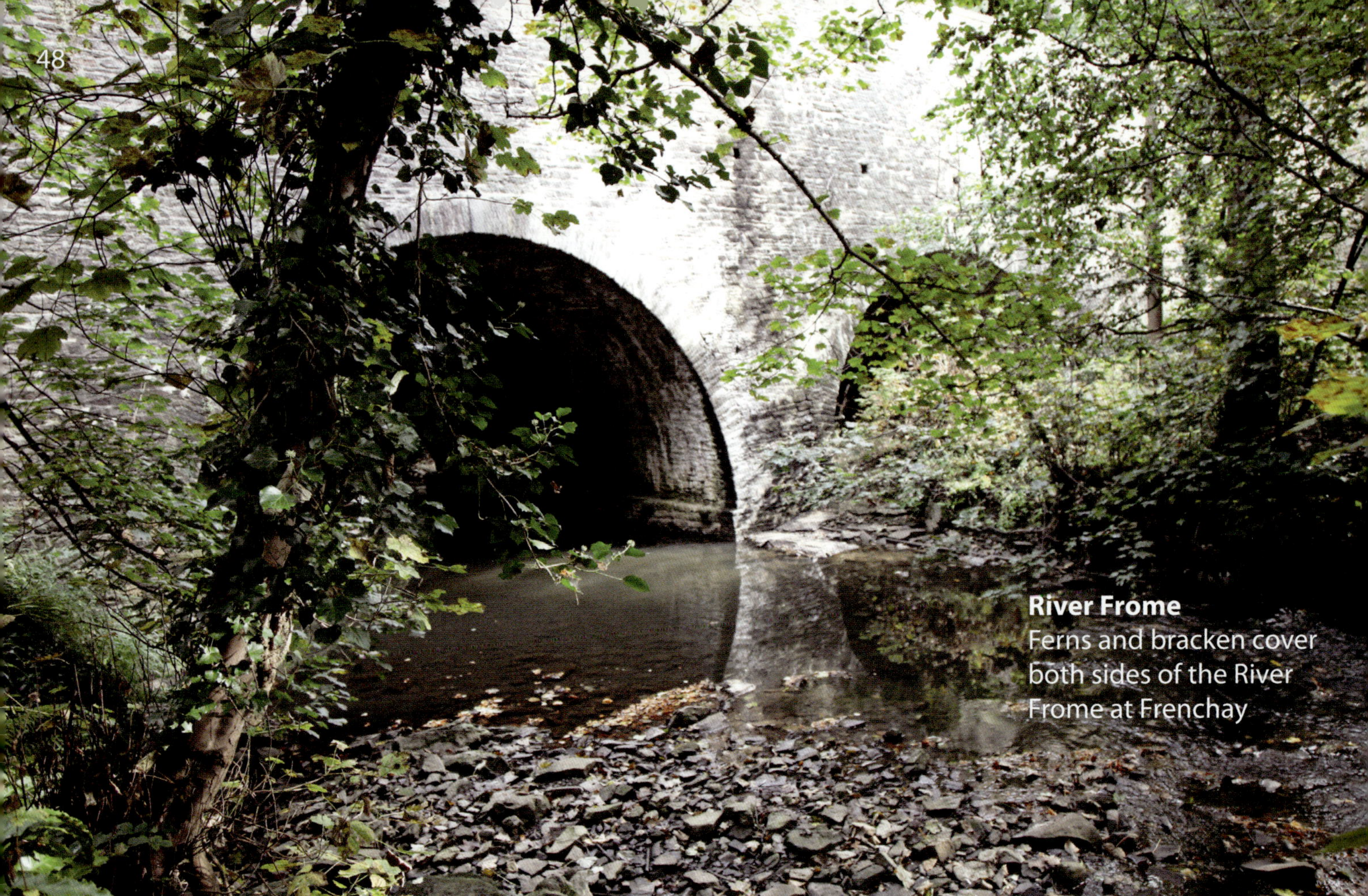

Damp places like this bridge on the River Frome at Frenchay are perfect places for ivy. If you look on the banks of the Frome you will also see ferns growing near the water's edge and in the nearby woods. The fronds emerge as curled tufts and grow into their feathery shapes: see page 51. These make great pictures. Britain's most widespread fern, bracken, can be found near the Frome where it forms attractive carpets in a few places.

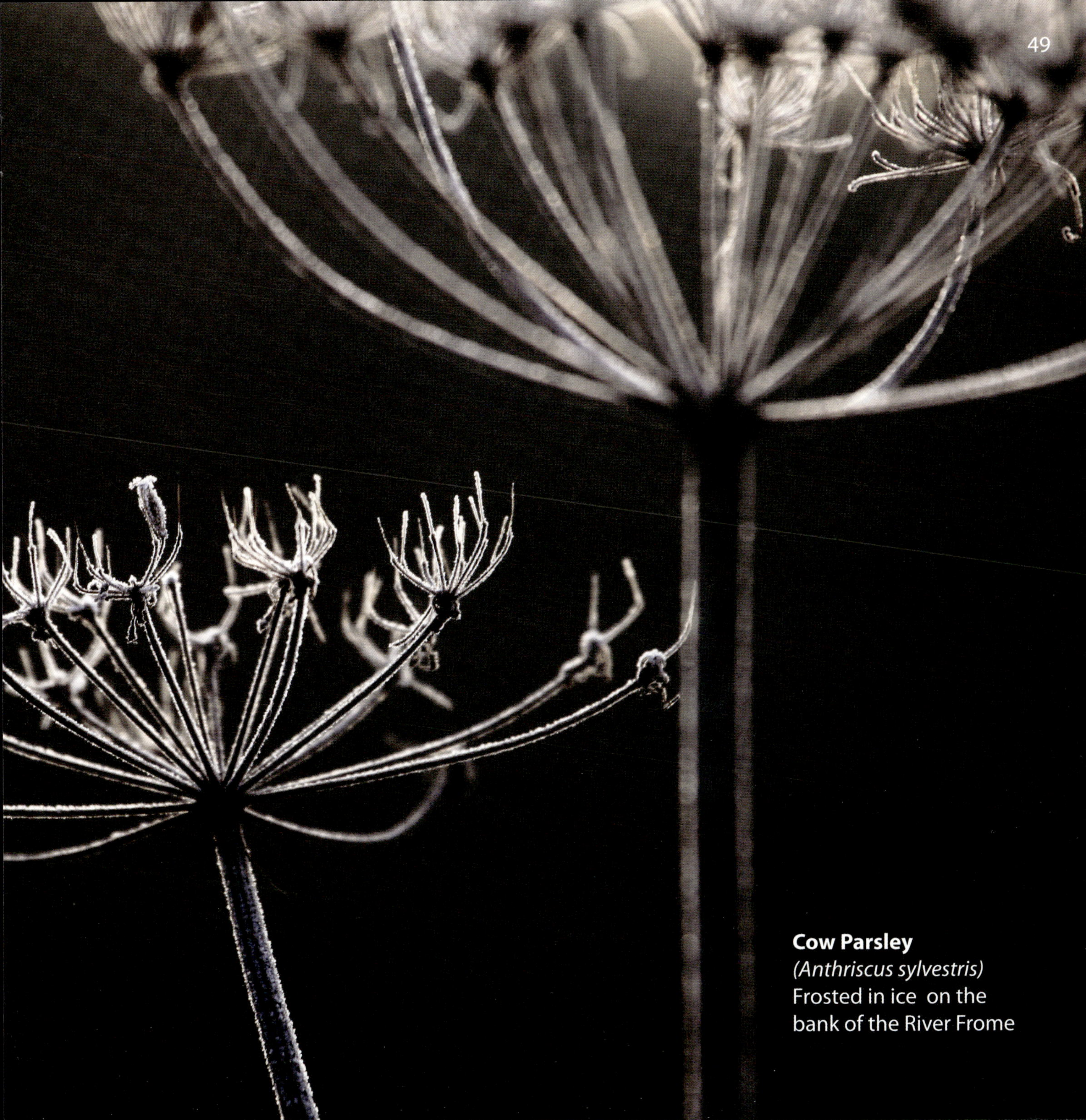

Cow Parsley
(Anthriscus sylvestris)
Frosted in ice on the
bank of the River Frome

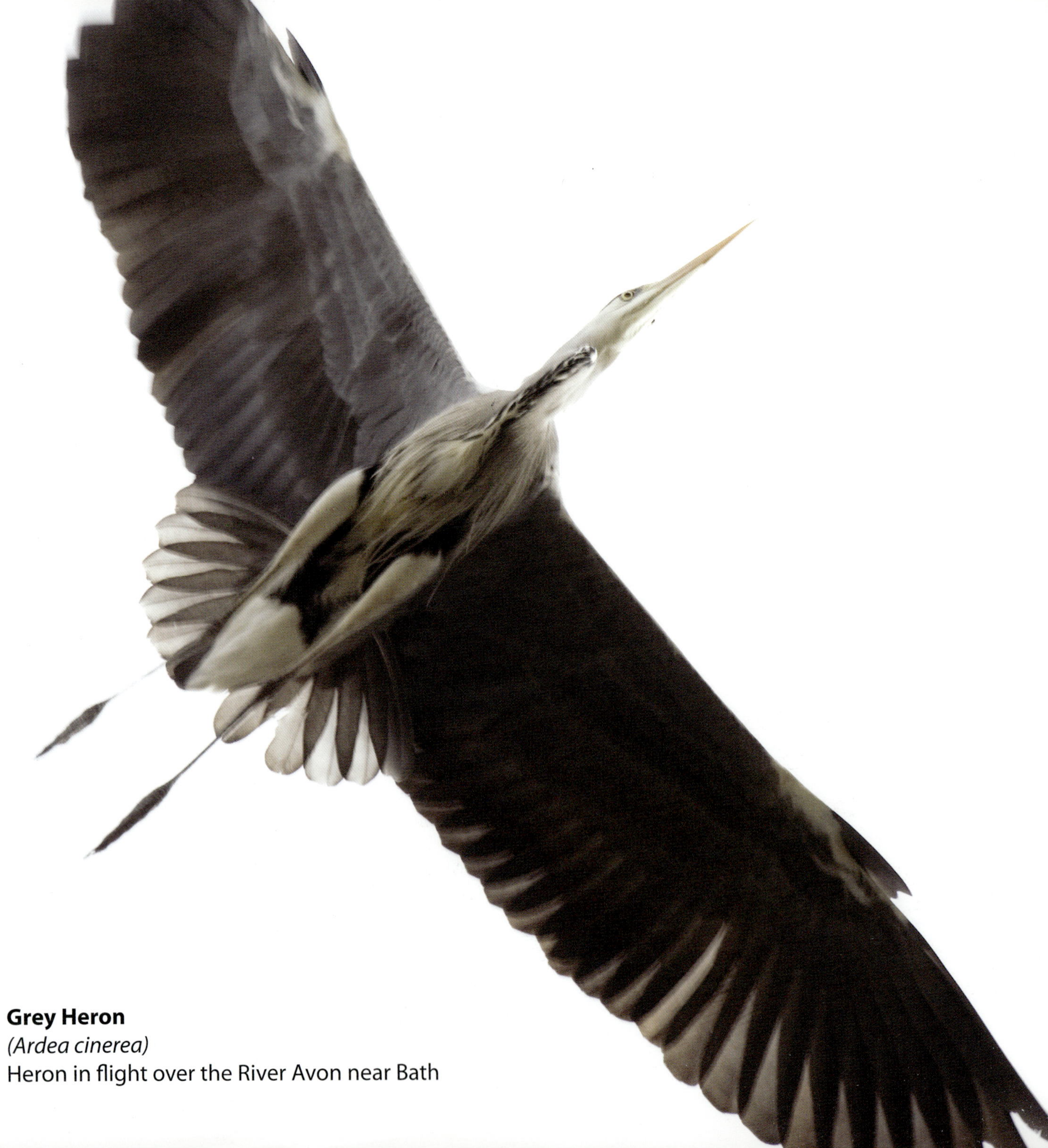

Grey Heron
(Ardea cinerea)
Heron in flight over the River Avon near Bath

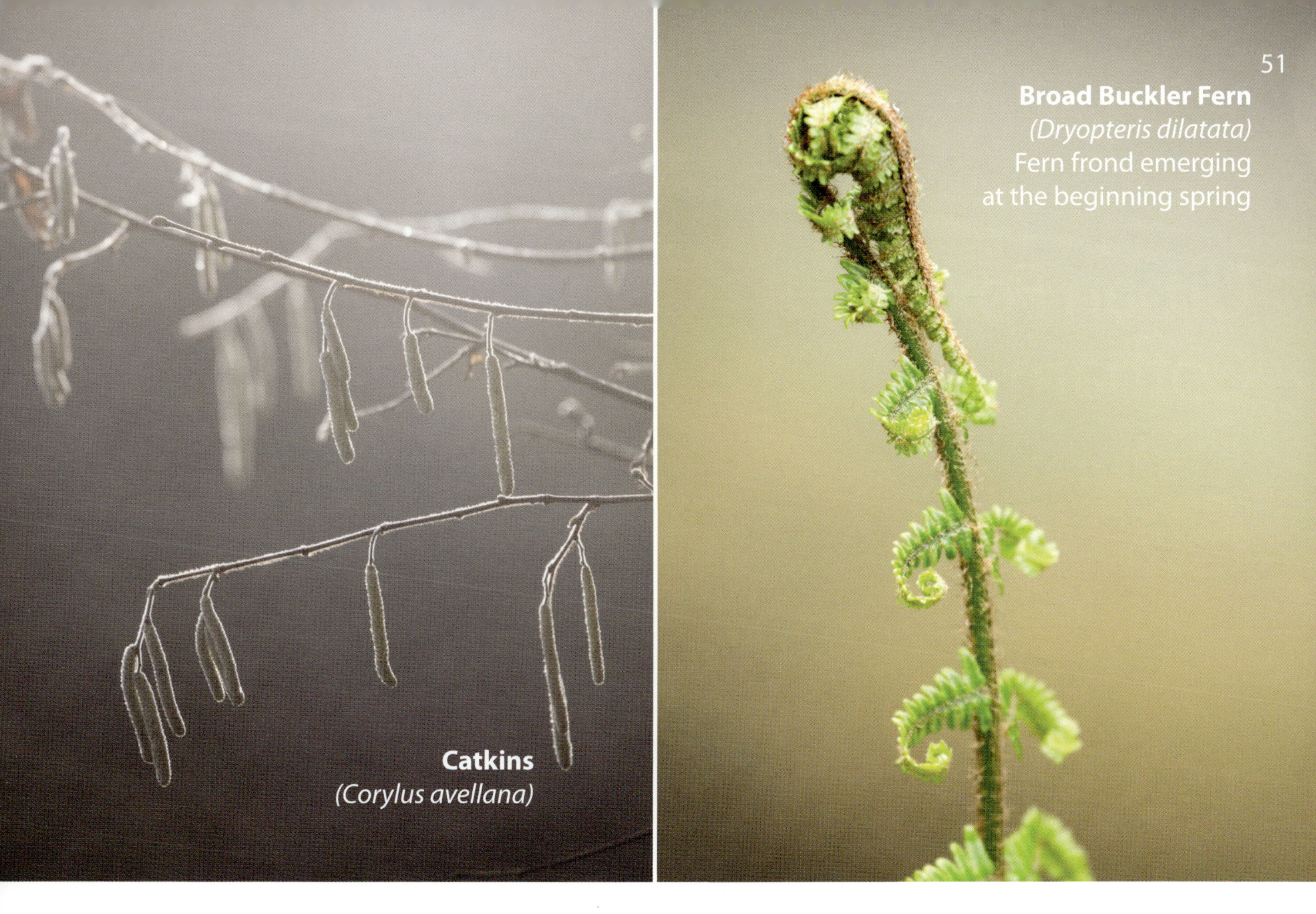

Go up the River Avon to near the city of Bath in February and March and look up towards the tree tops where you will see large nests taking shape with herons continually flying backwards and forwards with twigs and small branches in their beaks. Herons are easier to photograph and observe at this time of year as their minds are preoccupied. This area gets incredibly noisy – indeed deafening – when the chicks hatch. These birds return to the same nests each year so once you have found herons nesting you can come back each year at the same time to observe and photograph them. A trip to this stretch of river in the winter months is rewarding, especially at dawn or early morning as the mist is rolling off the water surface, creating a magical landscape.

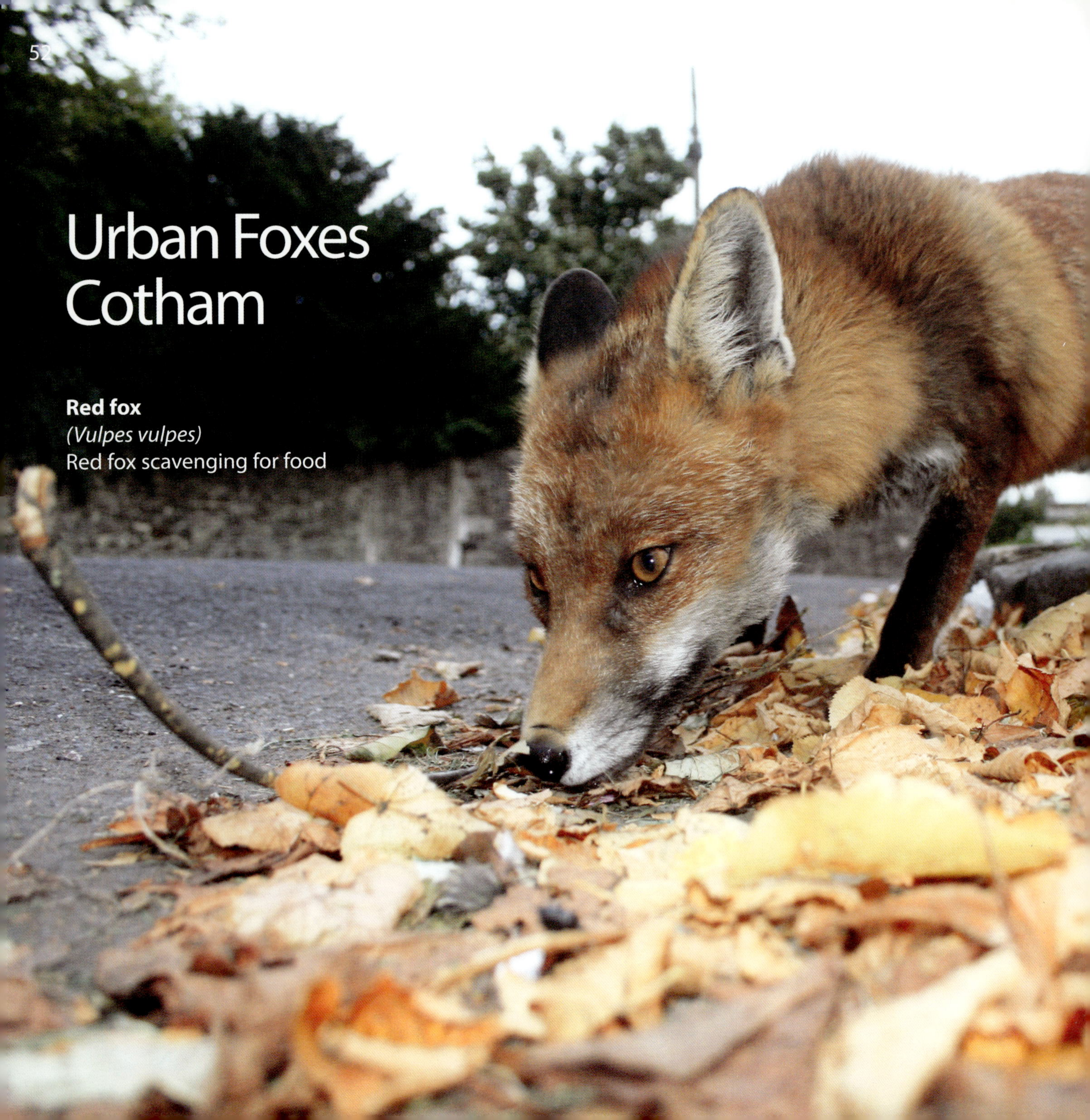

Urban Foxes
Cotham

Red fox
(Vulpes vulpes)
Red fox scavenging for food

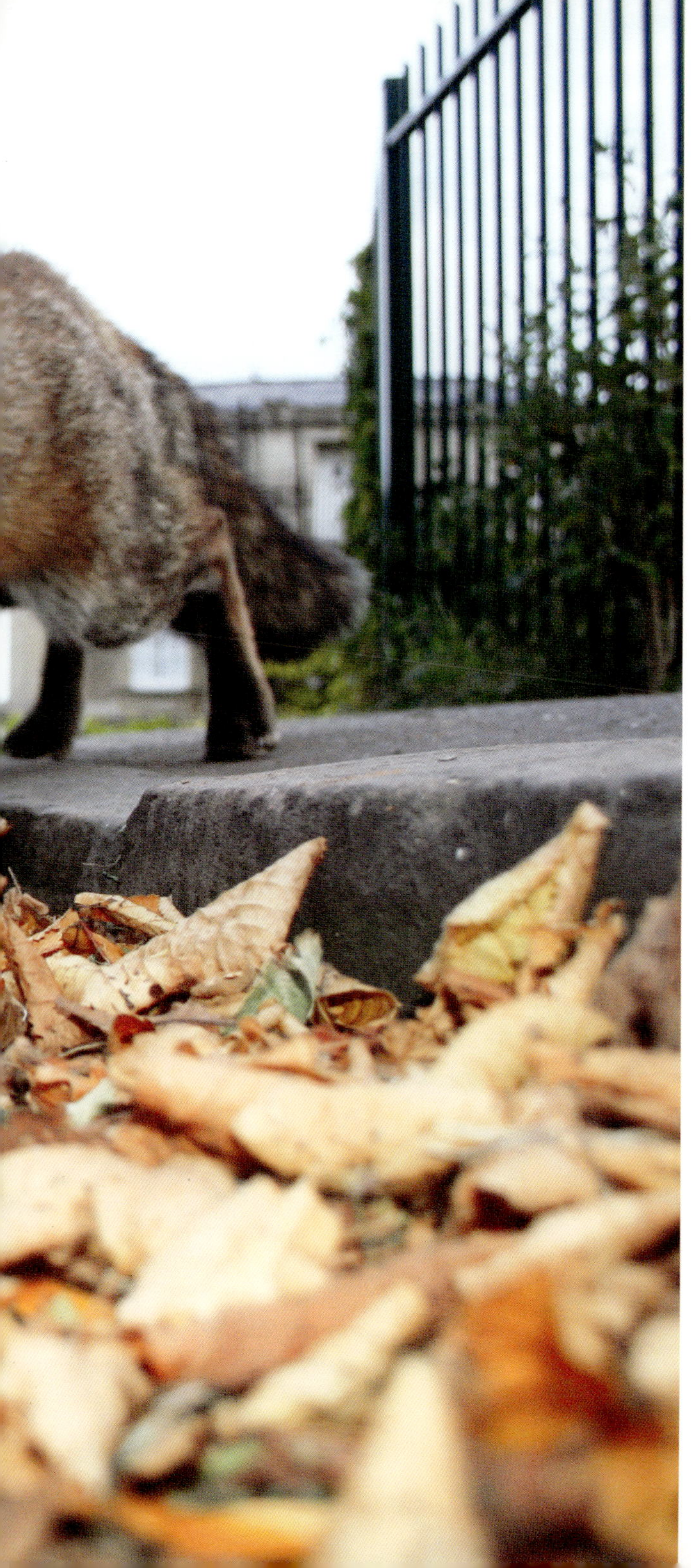

Ask any Bristolian which animal they associate with Bristol, and most would say the red fox. If you live in Bristol at some point you will stumble across a fox, almost literally. They are mostly nocturnal animals but can often be seen in the early morning or late evening. Bristol used to have one of the largest fox populations anywhere in the world but in 1996 mange, a skin disease, nearly wiped them out. Numbers had mostly recovered, but mange has been seen again in large numbers of Bristol's foxes.

Observing or photographing red foxes in the countryside is extremely hard. Once they pick up your scent they are usually long gone, but it's easier in the city. You would think most of the Bristol urban foxes would live on waste ground, allotments or churchyards, but surprisingly half of all earths are found in back gardens, especially under sheds and garages. Many people never know they are there! Foxes are at their most vocal in January when they begin the eerie mating calls, making for sleepless nights for many Bristolians.

In 1982 research showed that in Bristol in the densest fox-populated areas like Westbury-on-Trym, Cotham, Clifton and Kingswood there were up to 10 families of foxes to every square mile.

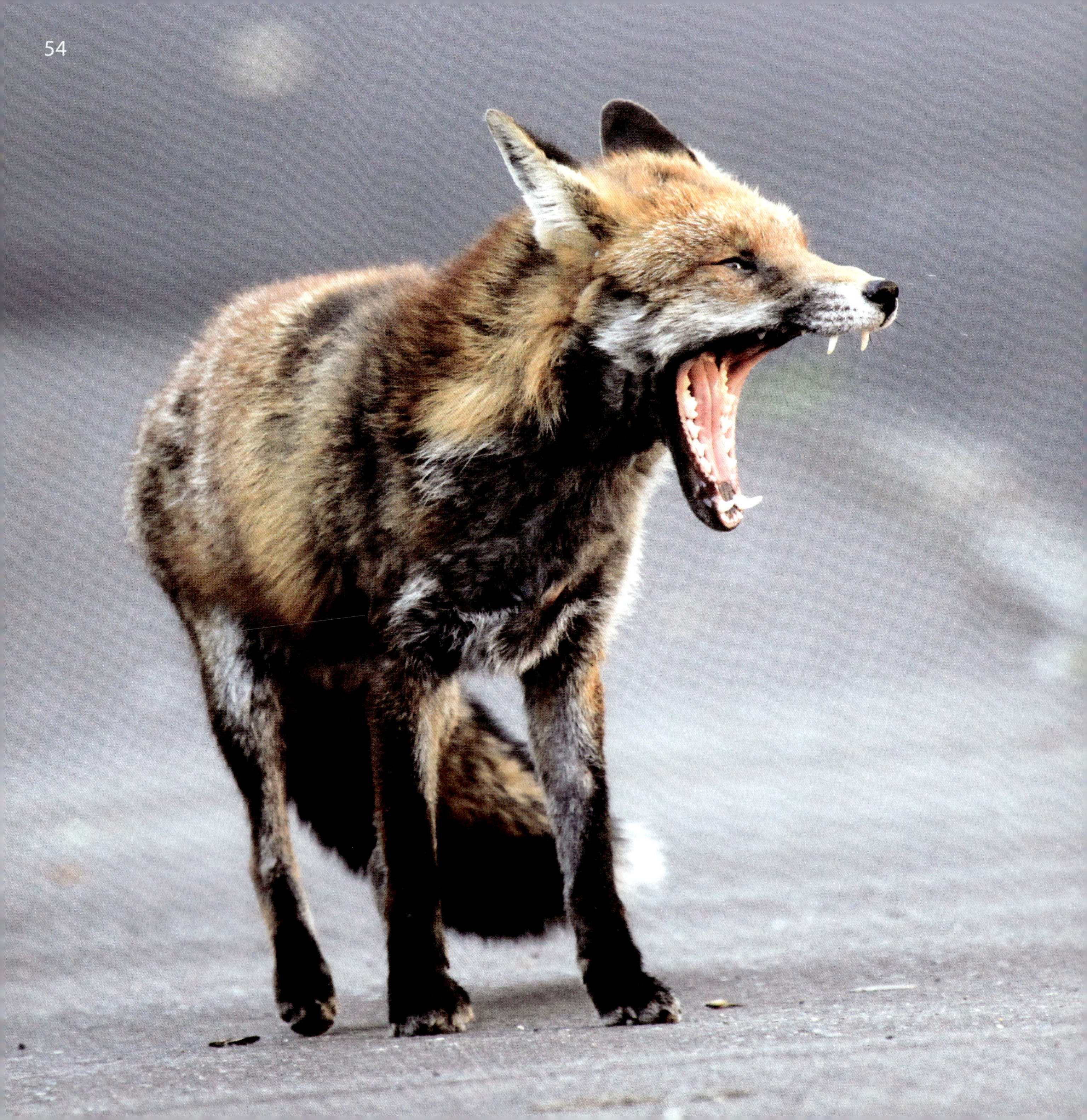

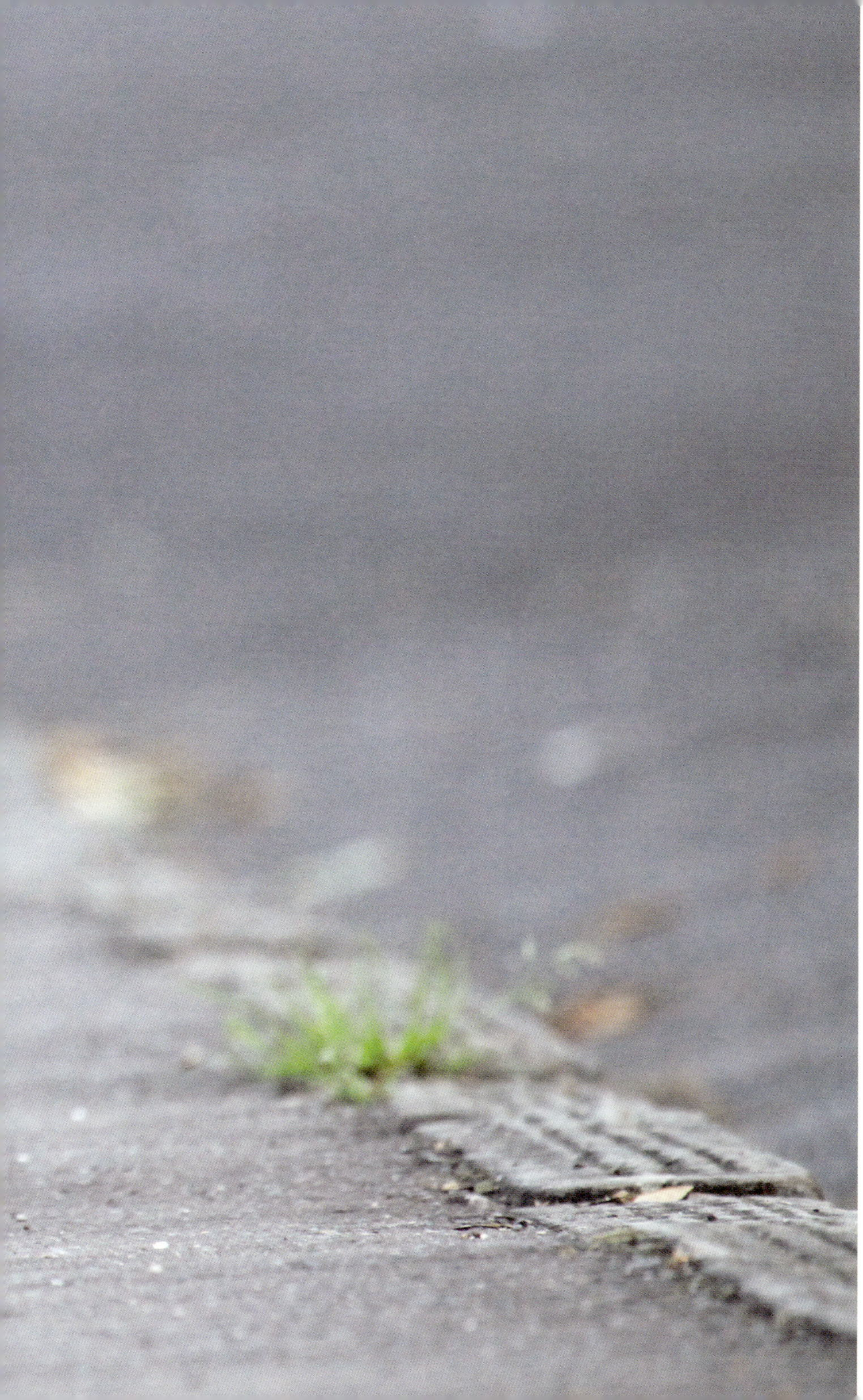

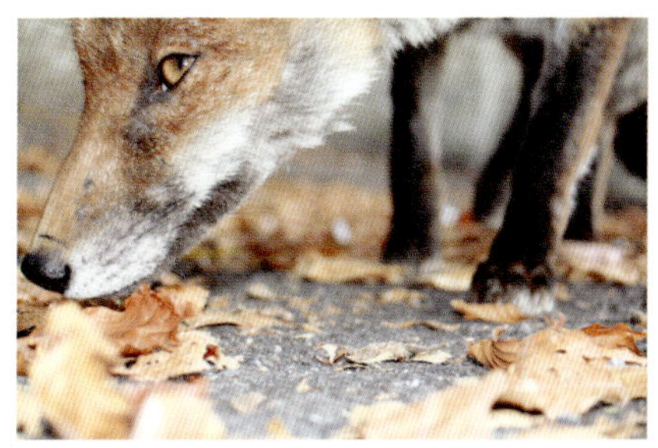

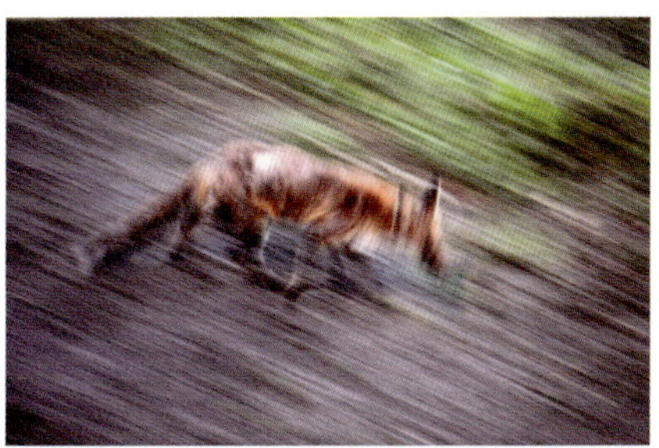

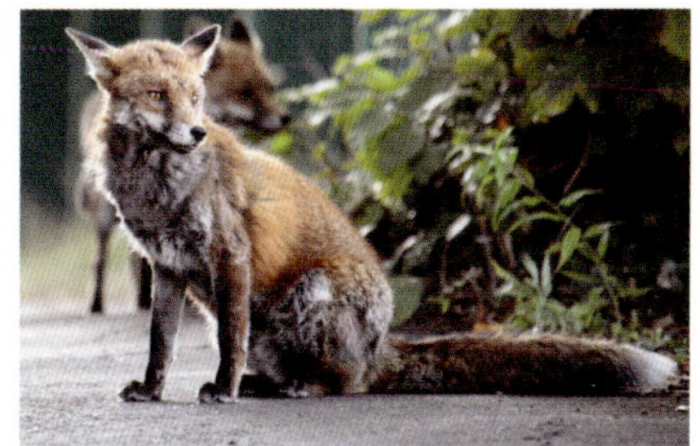

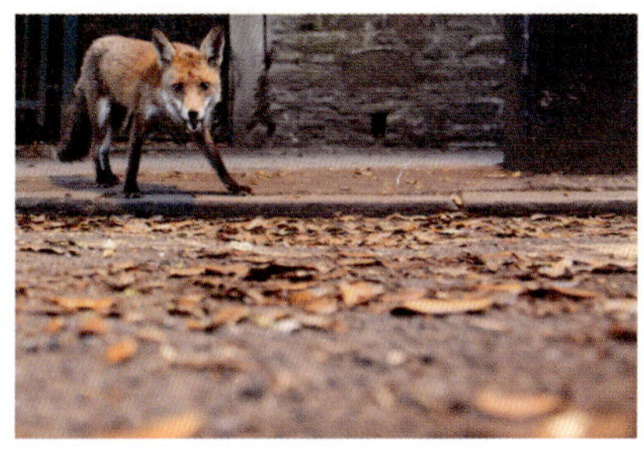

Red Fox
(Vulpes vulpes)
Dog fox active during
daylight in Bristol

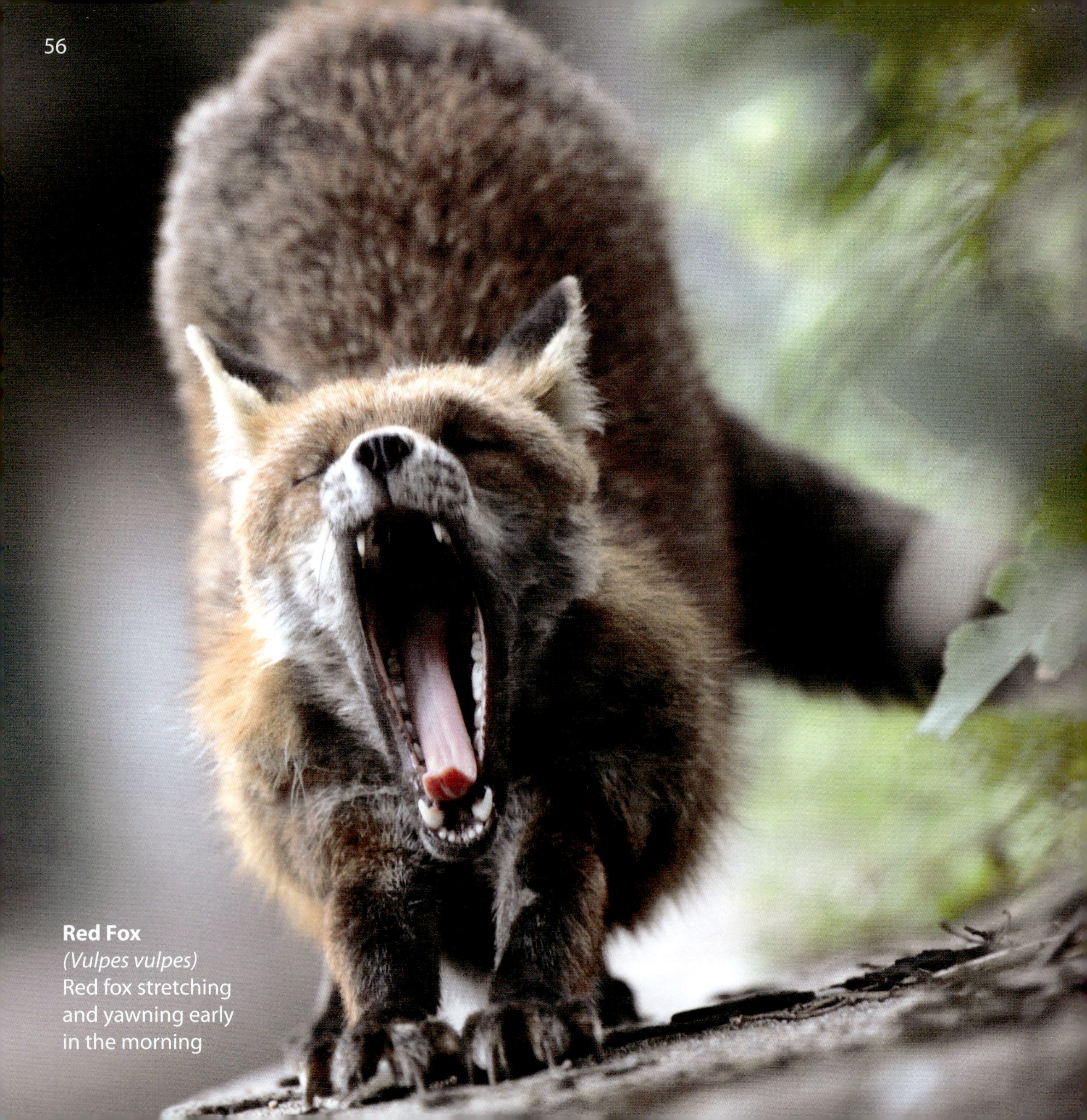

Red Fox
(Vulpes vulpes)
Red fox stretching
and yawning early
in the morning

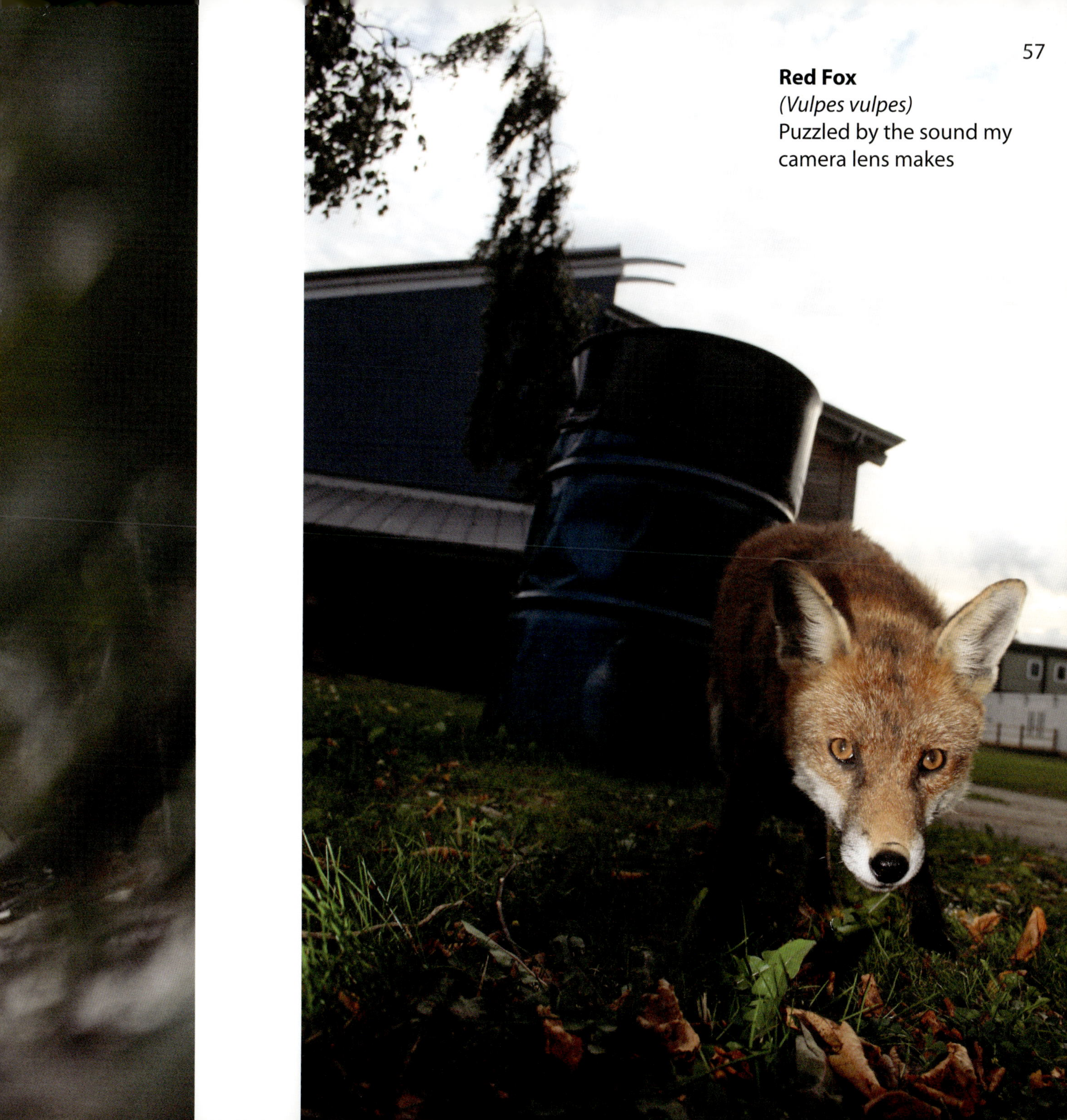

Red Fox
(Vulpes vulpes)
Puzzled by the sound my
camera lens makes

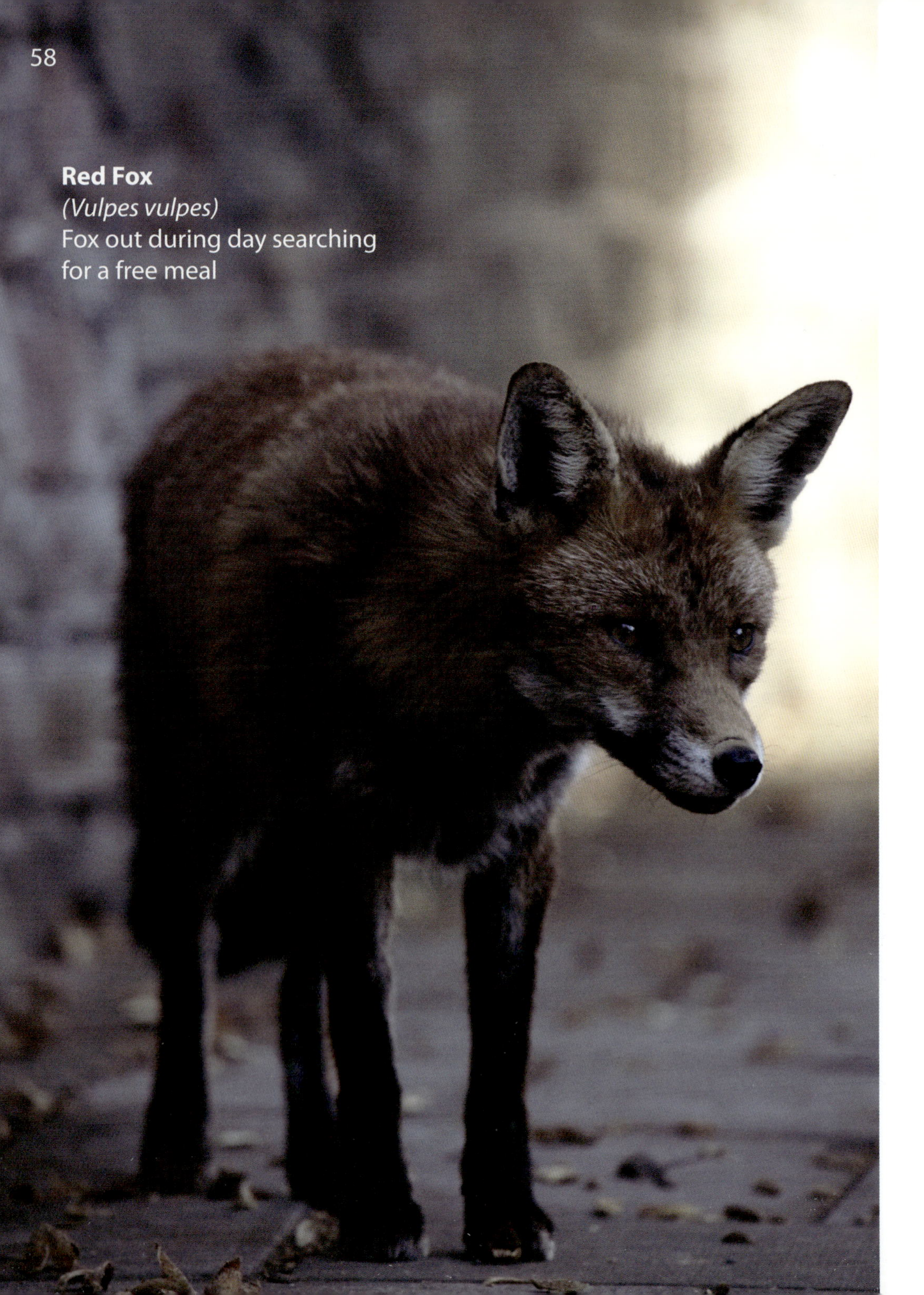

Red Fox
(Vulpes vulpes)
Fox out during day searching
for a free meal

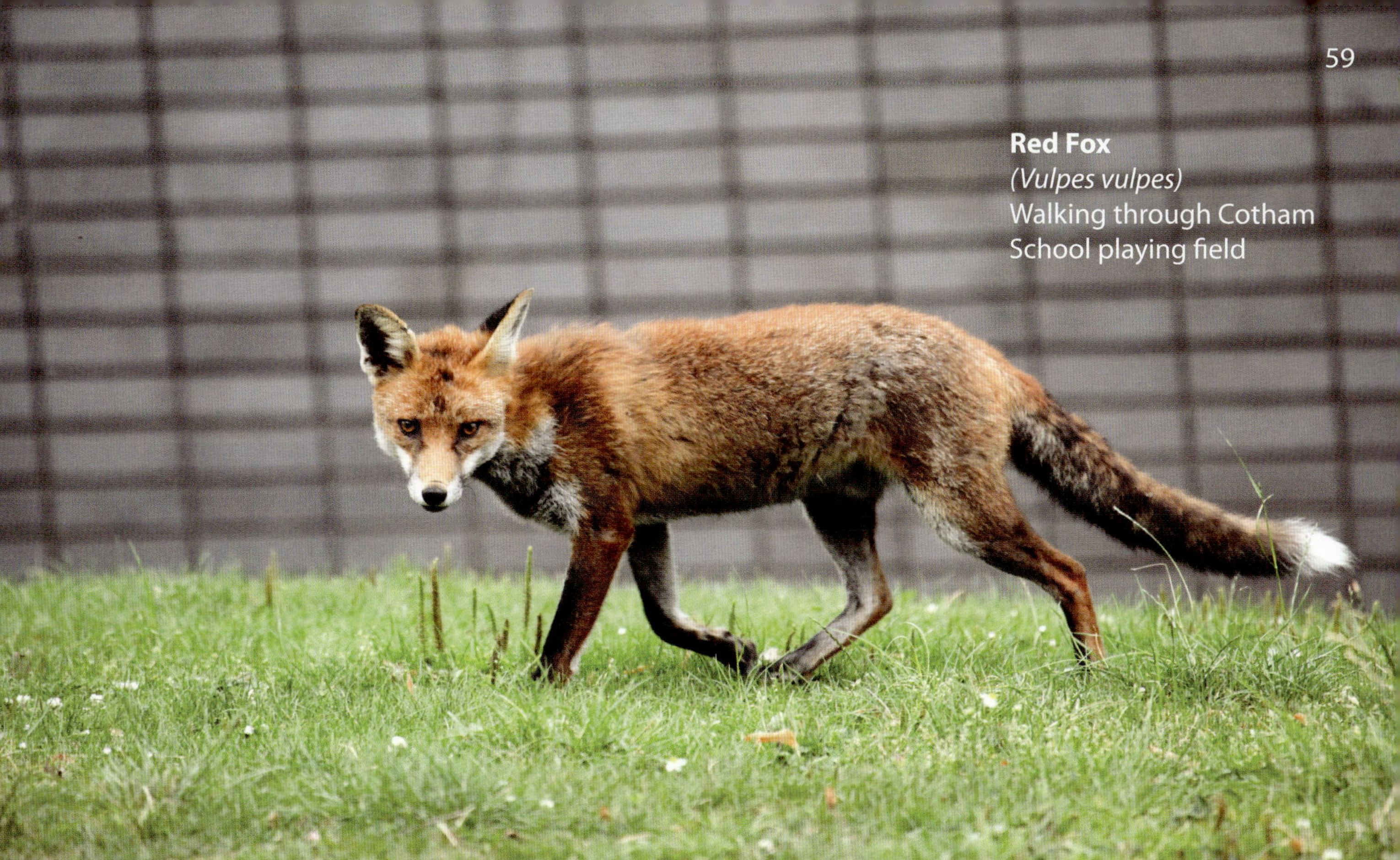

Having recently spent most of my spare time before and after work observing and photographing two families of urban foxes living in the same location in Cotham I was taken aback by how intelligent these animals are. There were two vixens and one dog fox with three cubs. I nicknamed one of these foxes Fearless Freddy. This dog fox was fascinating to watch and seemed intrigued by the presence of human company. It seemed locals living in this street were really fond of the animal.

Over the months I photographed this particular fox I always felt safe and at times he would sit next to me and sometimes fall asleep. Foxes are loved and hated in equal measure. I have been threatened while taking photographs and on one occasion people contacted the local paper to complain. One day a driver in a car spotted the fox I was photographing and tried to run it over, only missing by inches.

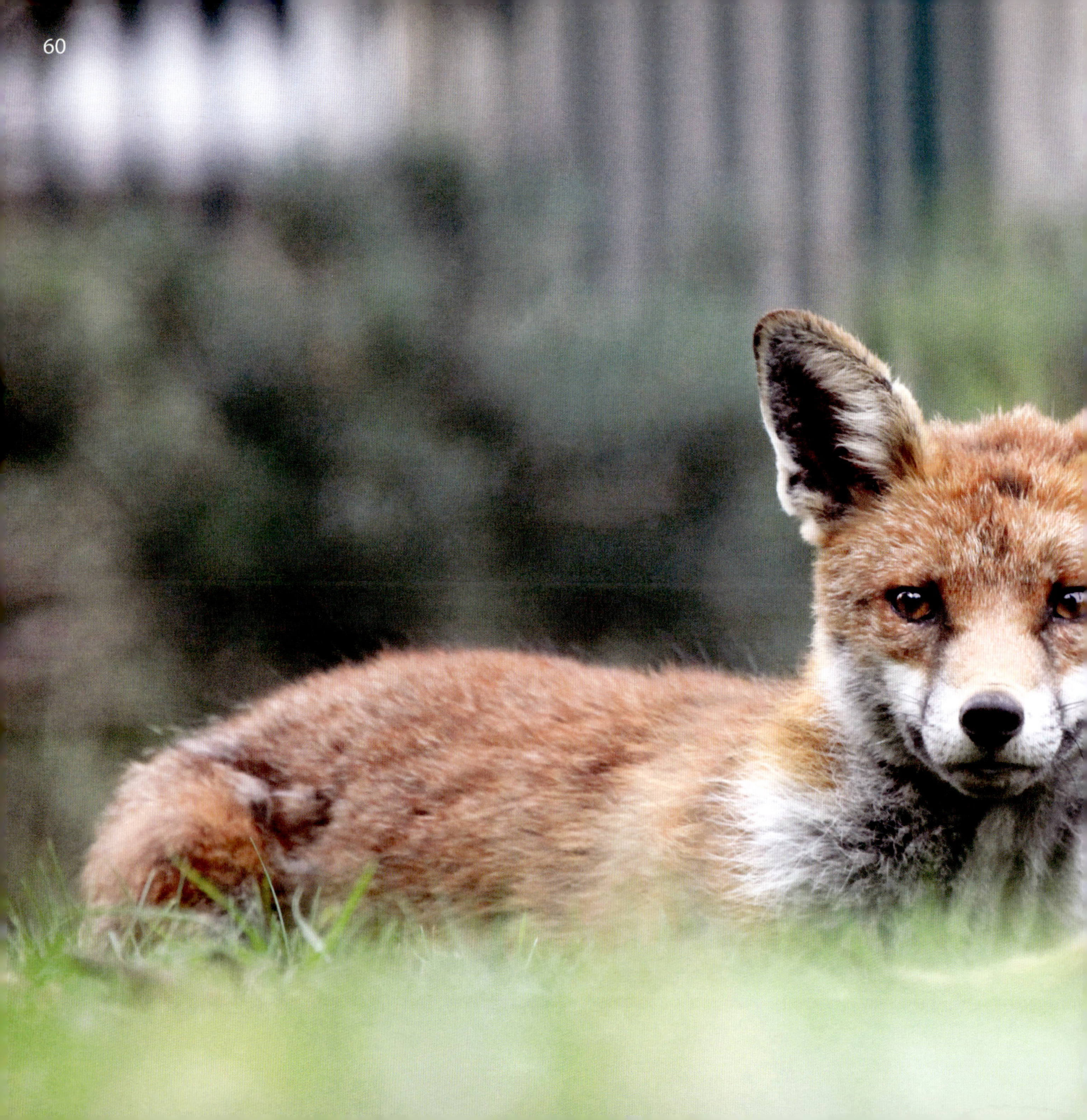

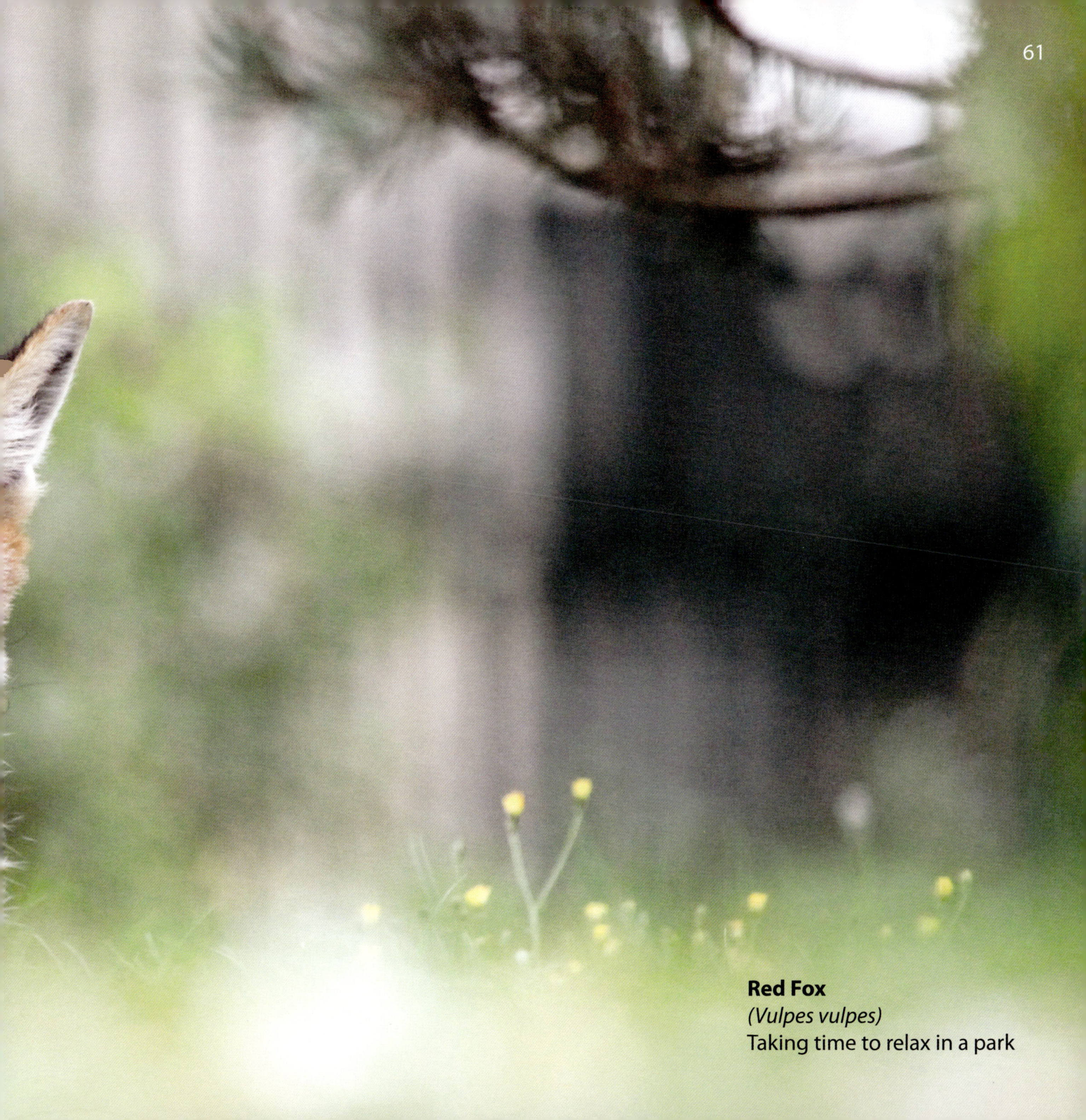

Red Fox
(Vulpes vulpes)
Taking time to relax in a park

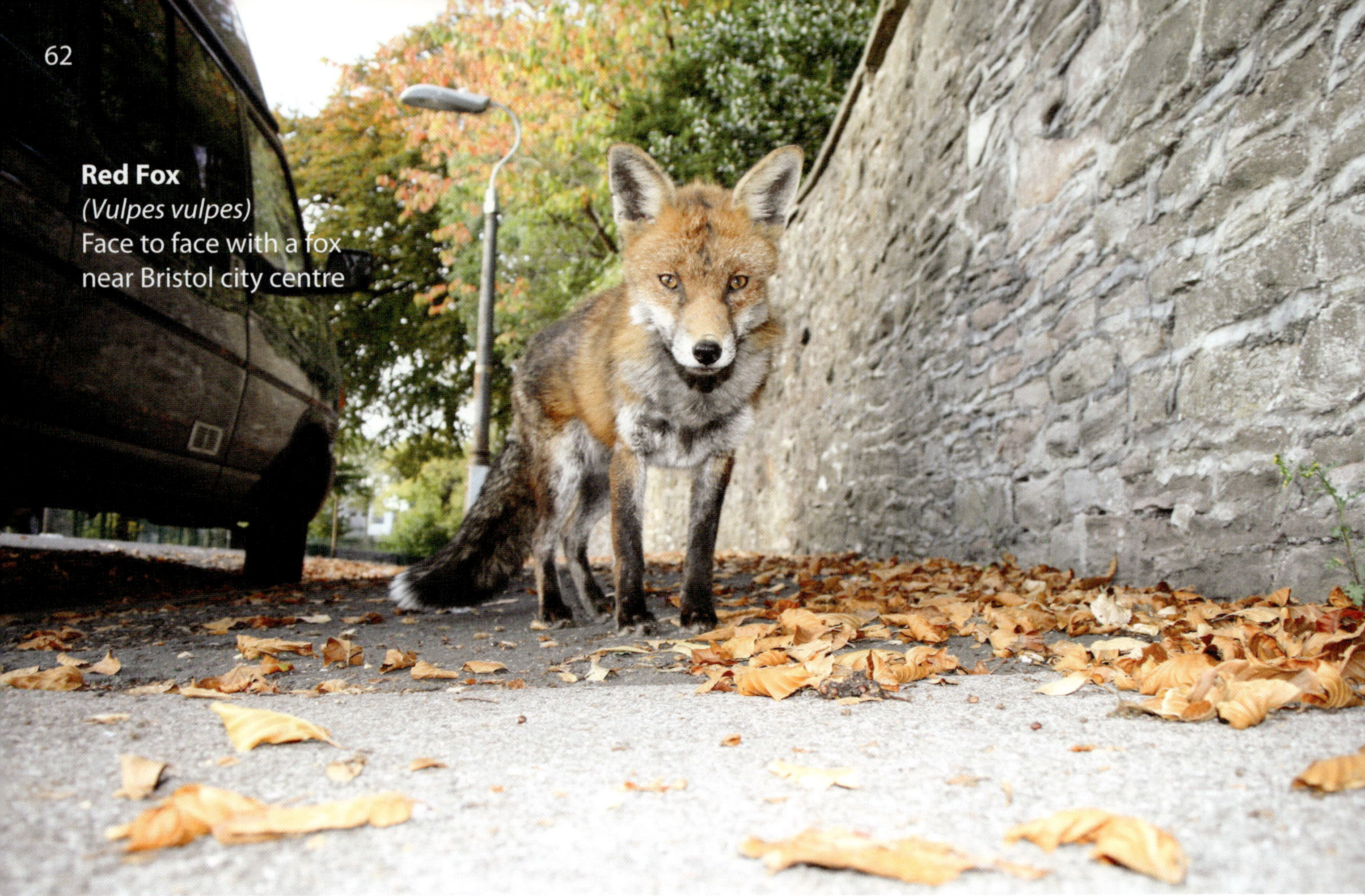

Despite this occasional hostility, urban foxes have an easier time of it than their country cousins. It's easier to eat the left-overs from humans than to hunt and stalk prey. The city landscape is perfect for a fox. The biggest problem urban foxes have is traffic and canine mange. Foxes usually have 4-5 pups, born in spring, so keep an eye out at this time and you could be lucky enough to see a family of foxes going about their business in the centre of our city.

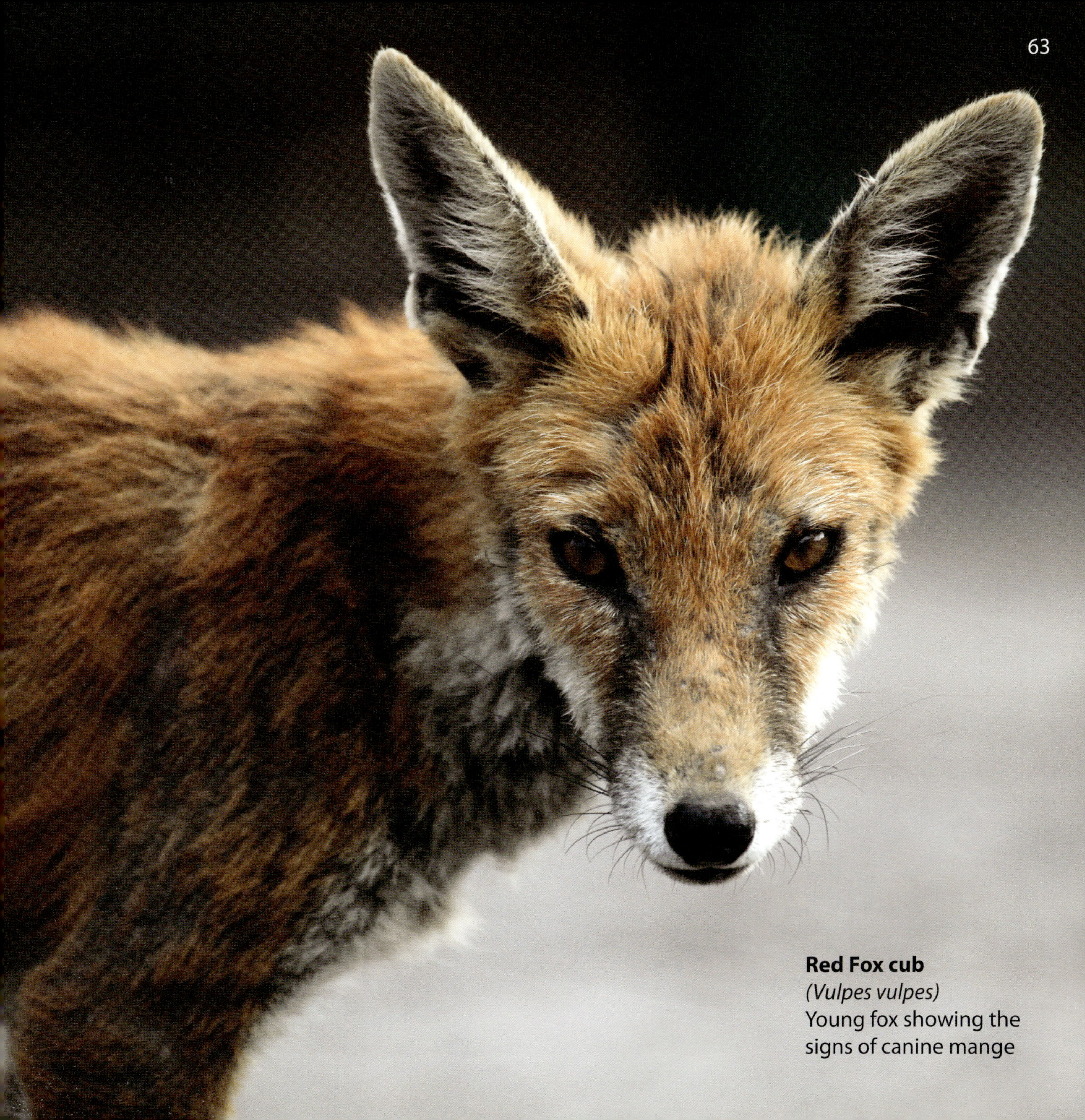

Red Fox cub
(Vulpes vulpes)
Young fox showing the
signs of canine mange

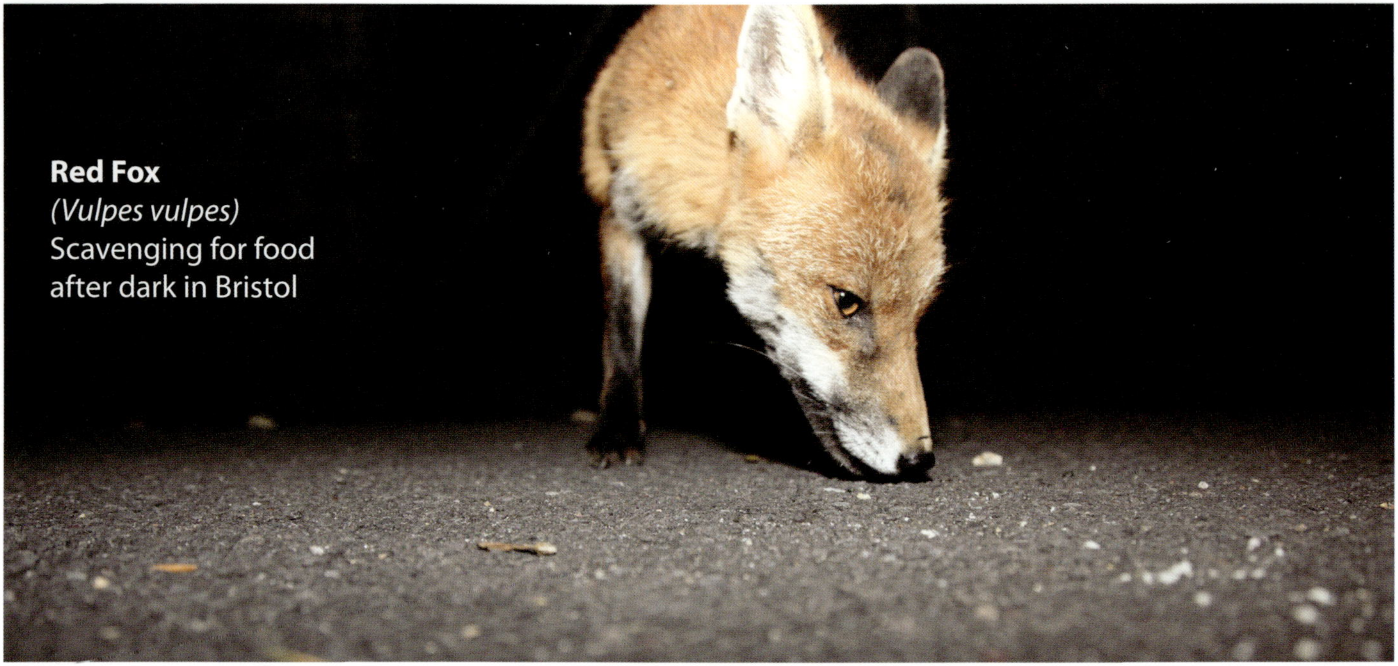

Red Fox
(Vulpes vulpes)
Scavenging for food
after dark in Bristol

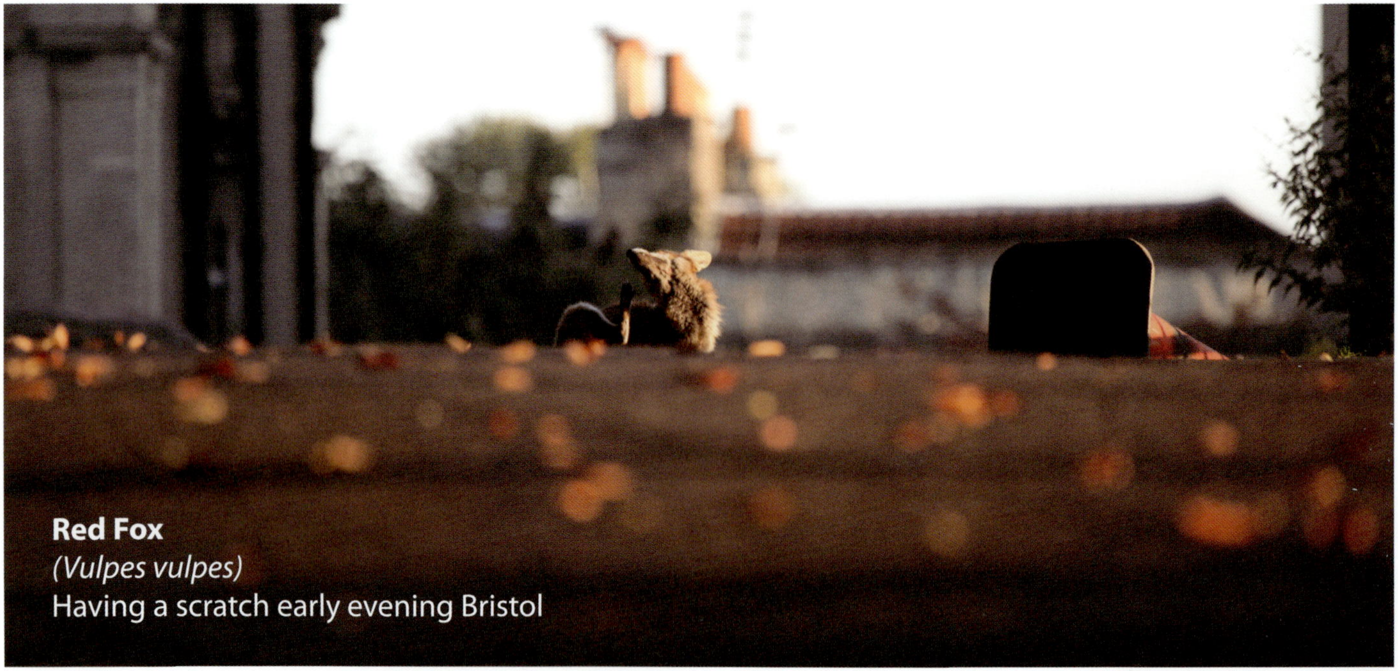

Red Fox
(Vulpes vulpes)
Having a scratch early evening Bristol

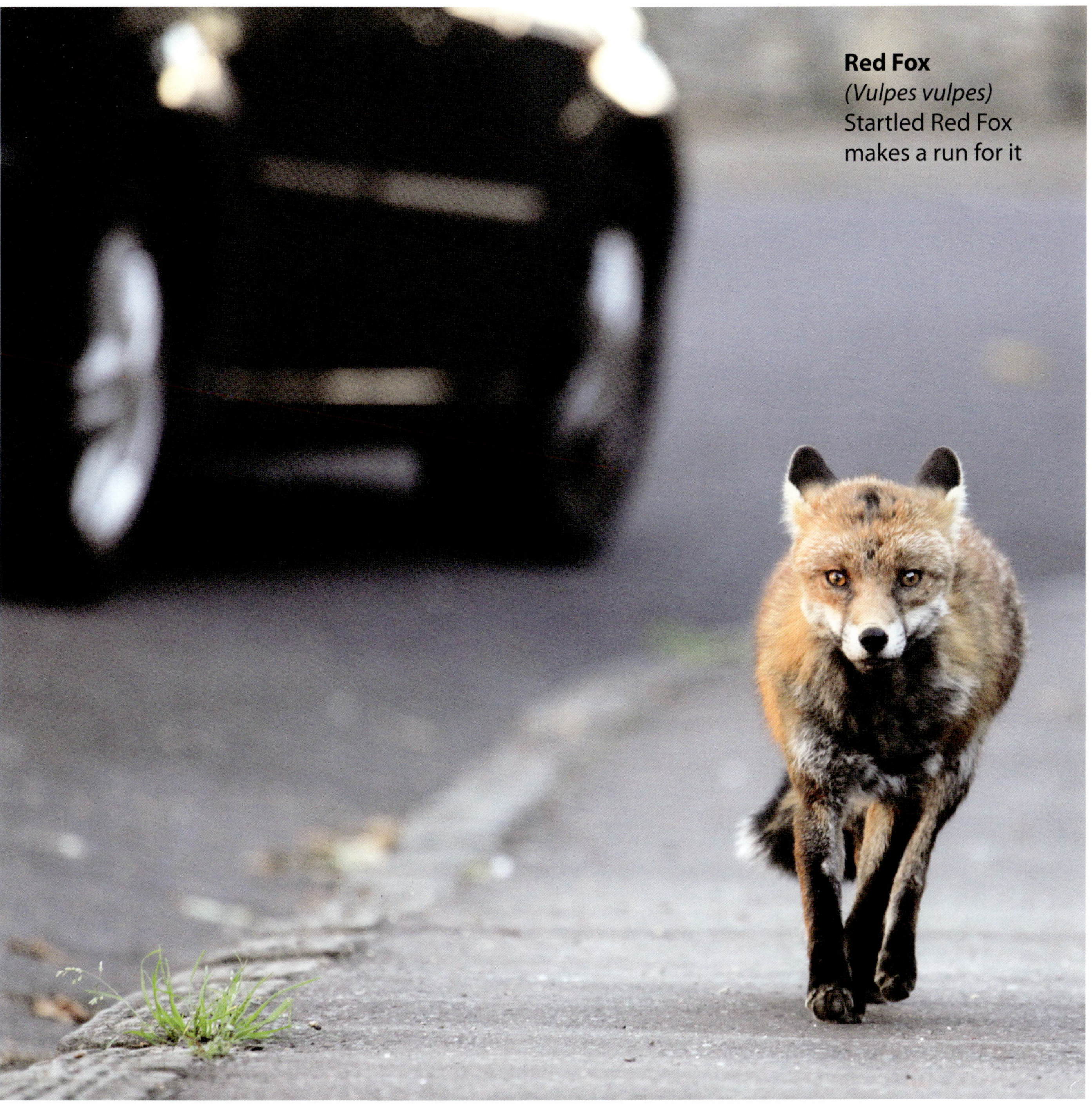

Red Fox
(Vulpes vulpes)
Startled Red Fox
makes a run for it

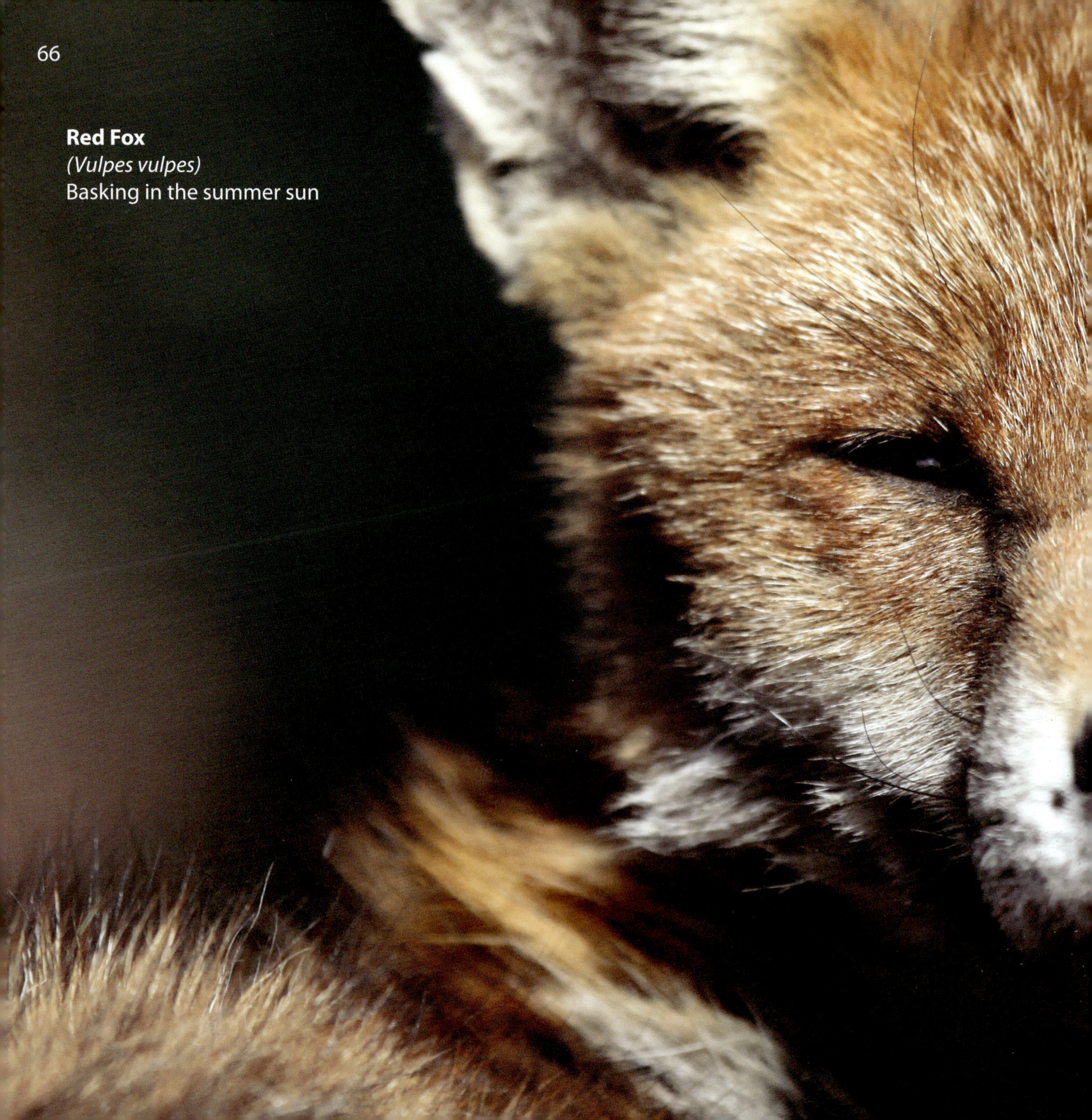

Red Fox
(Vulpes vulpes)
Basking in the summer sun

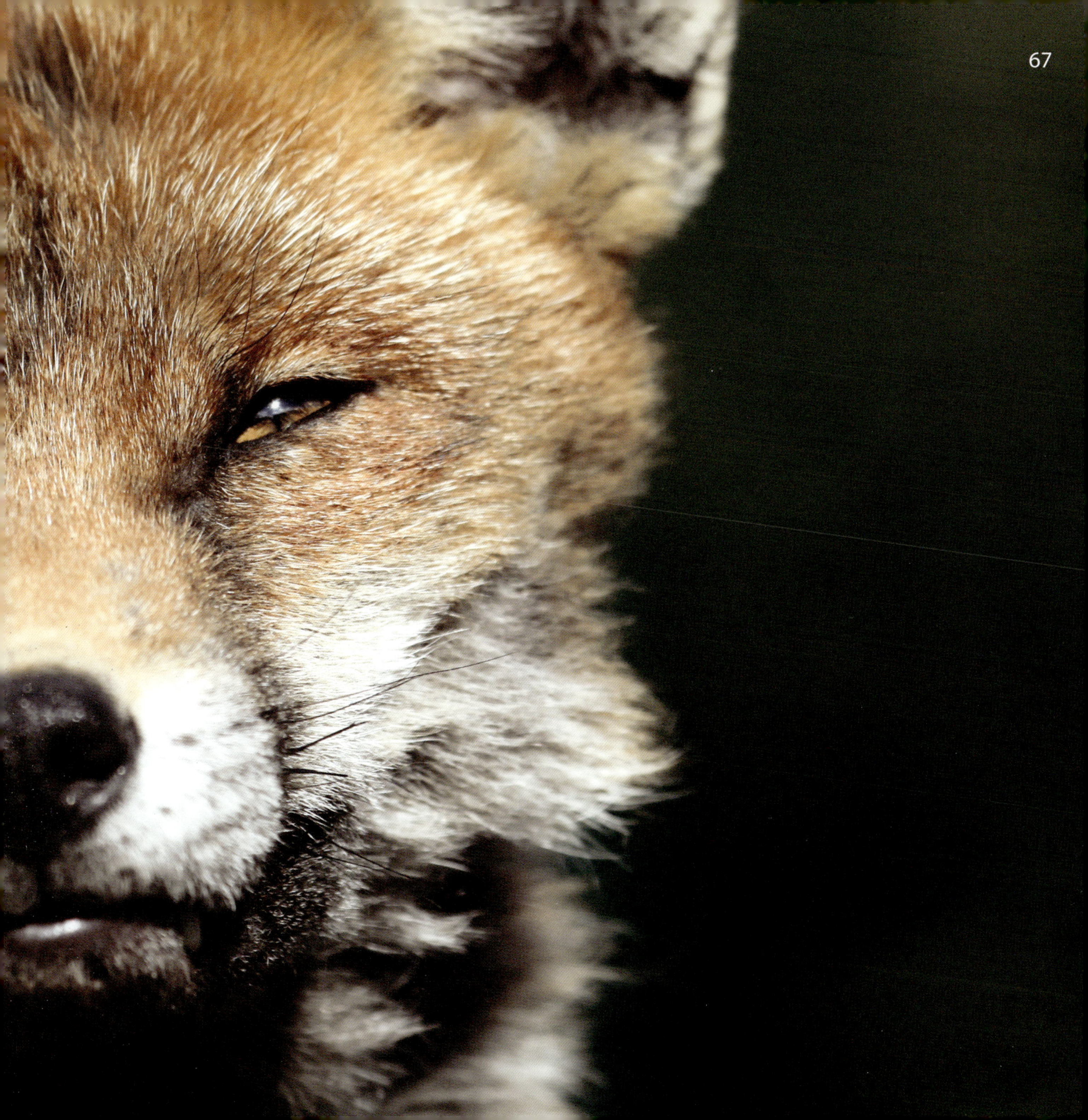

Bedminster Down

Lesser Black-backed Gull
(Larus fuscus)
Bedminster roof top in
West Street

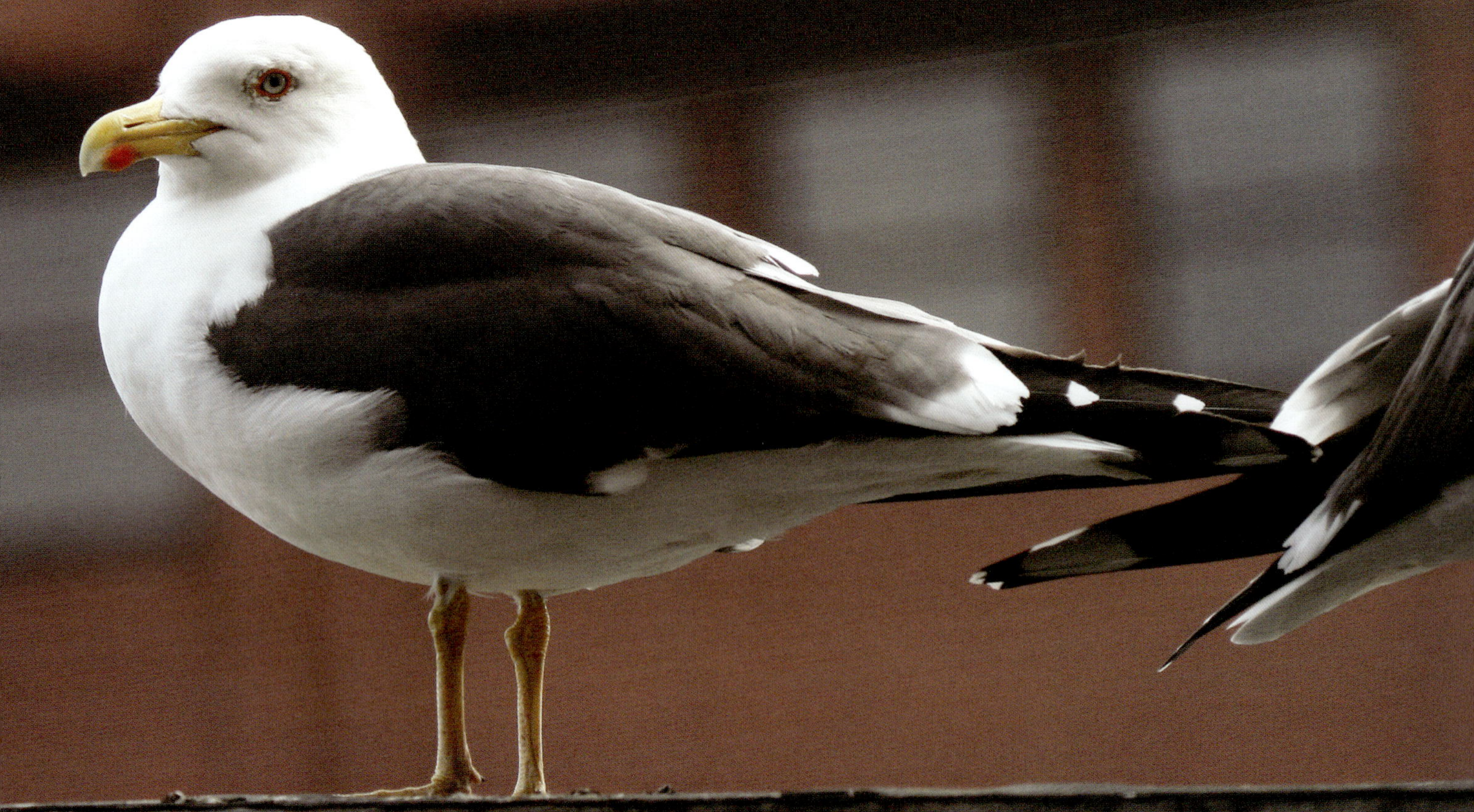

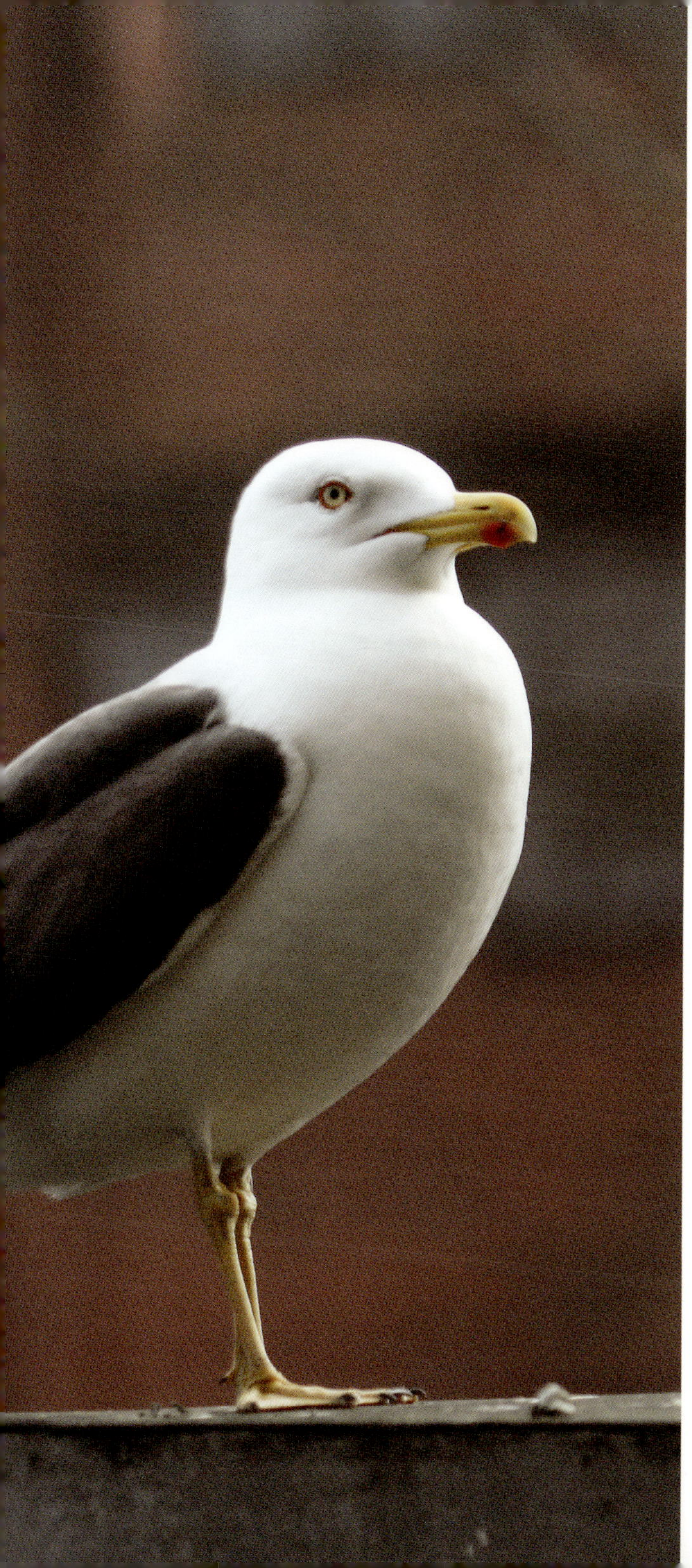

Bedminster Down might not be a place you would readily associate with urban wildlife but there is a surprising amount there. Healthy numbers of rabbits live in burrows just off the main road through Bedminster Down. And where there are rabbits there will always be a bird of prey or two. Buzzards fly high on a summer's evening over the rabbits waiting for a young one to stray away from the safety of its family. Gulls, black-headed and lesser black-backed, feed on waste, and worms and insects which are plentiful in this area.

If you see a gull on a grassy area watch out for typical gull behaviour. This is called dancing for their dinner, as the bird mimics rain drops on the water surface in an attempt to draw the worms to the surface.

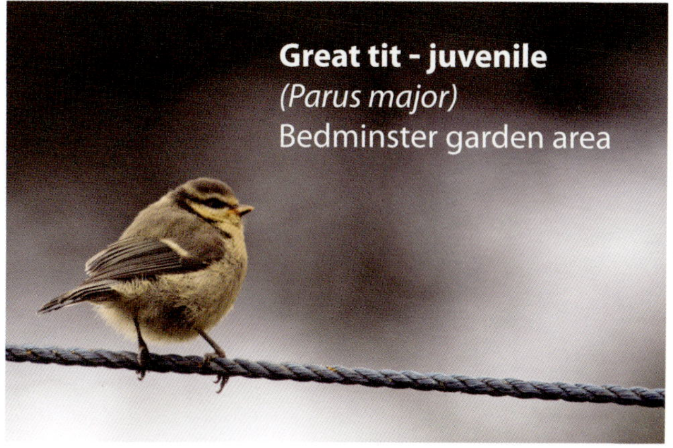

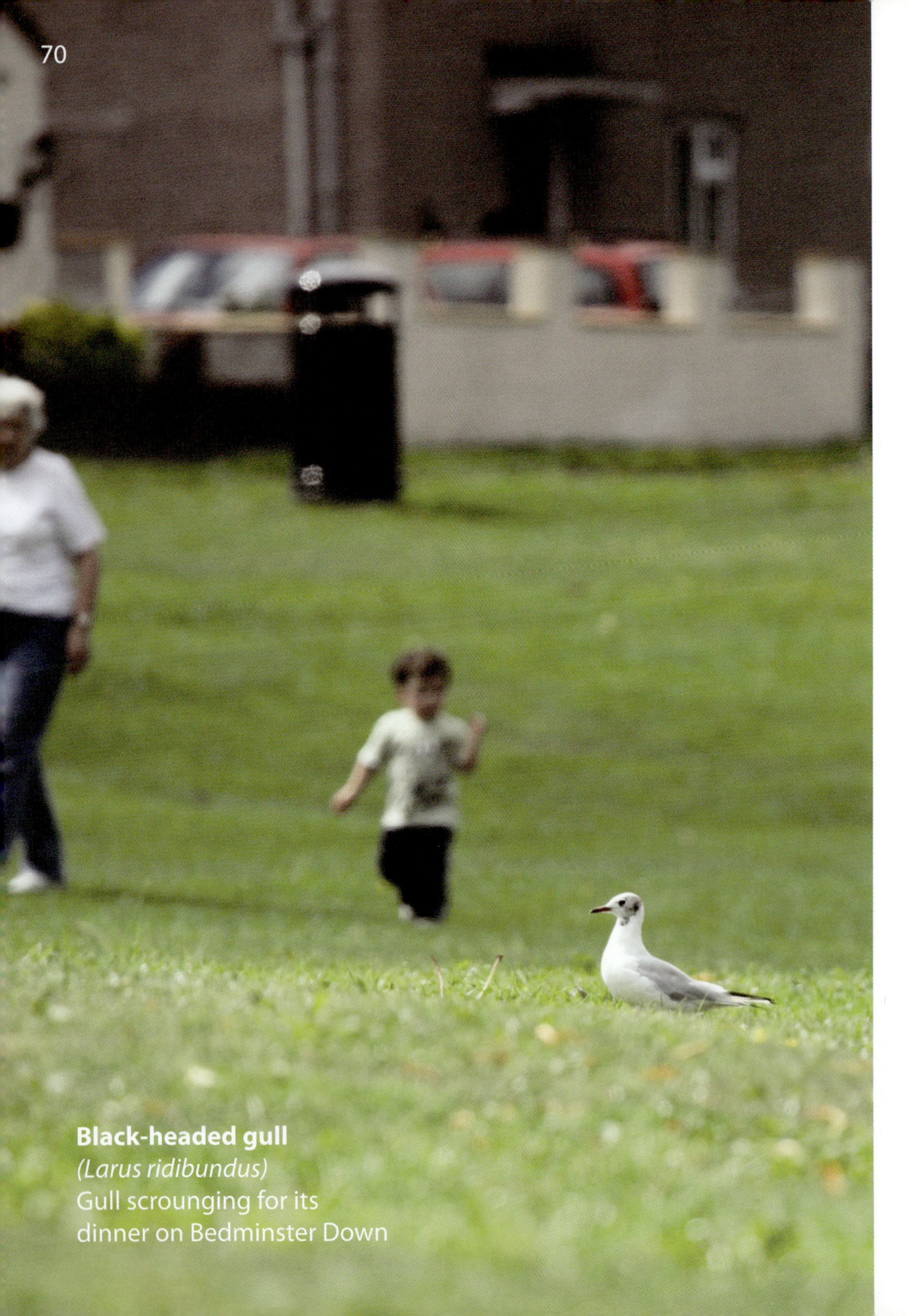

Black-headed gull
(Larus ridibundus)
Gull scrounging for its
dinner on Bedminster Down

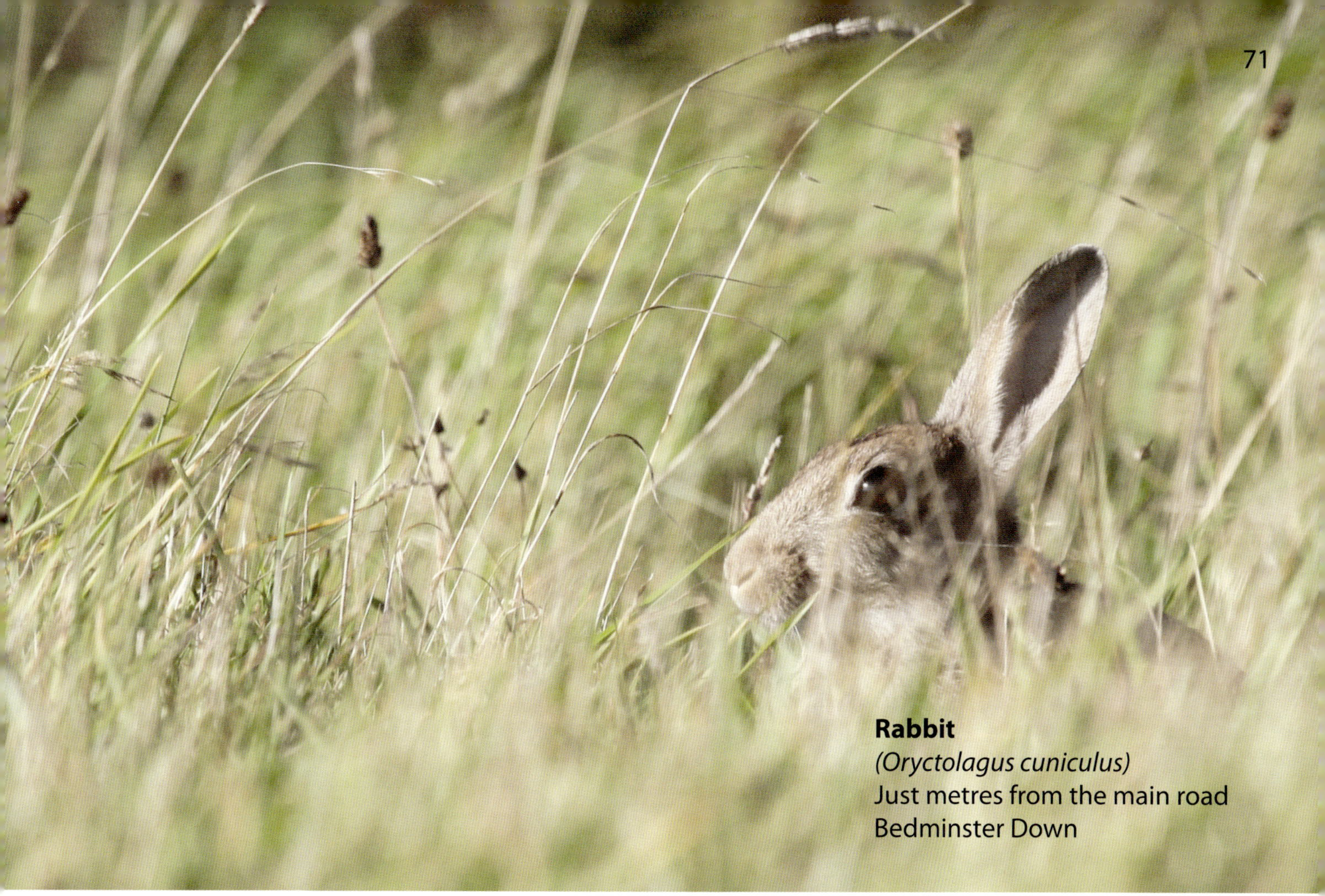

Rabbit
(*Oryctolagus cuniculus*)
Just metres from the main road
Bedminster Down

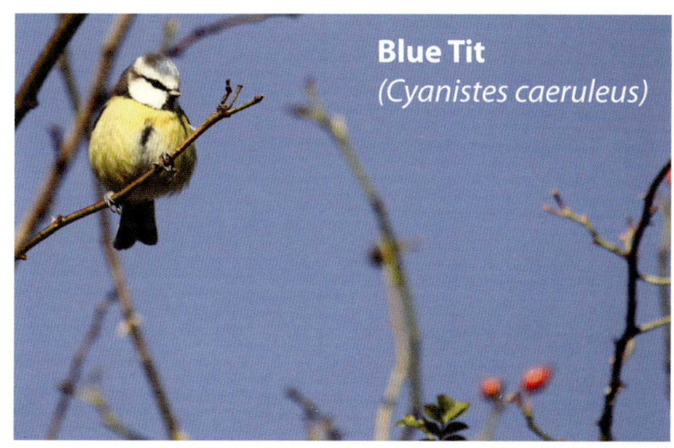

Blue Tit
(*Cyanistes caeruleus*)

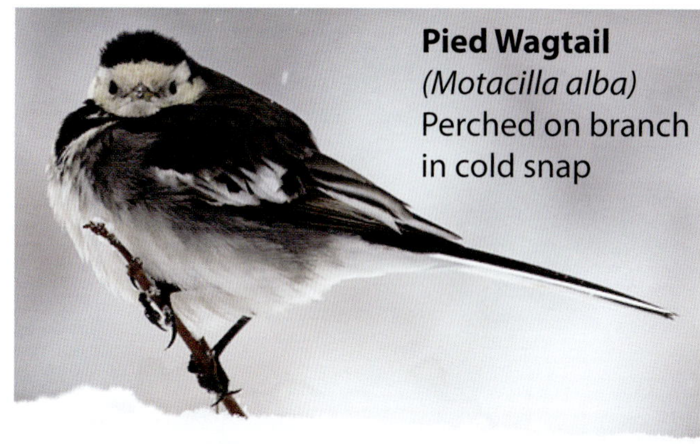

Pied Wagtail
(*Motacilla alba*)
Perched on branch
in cold snap

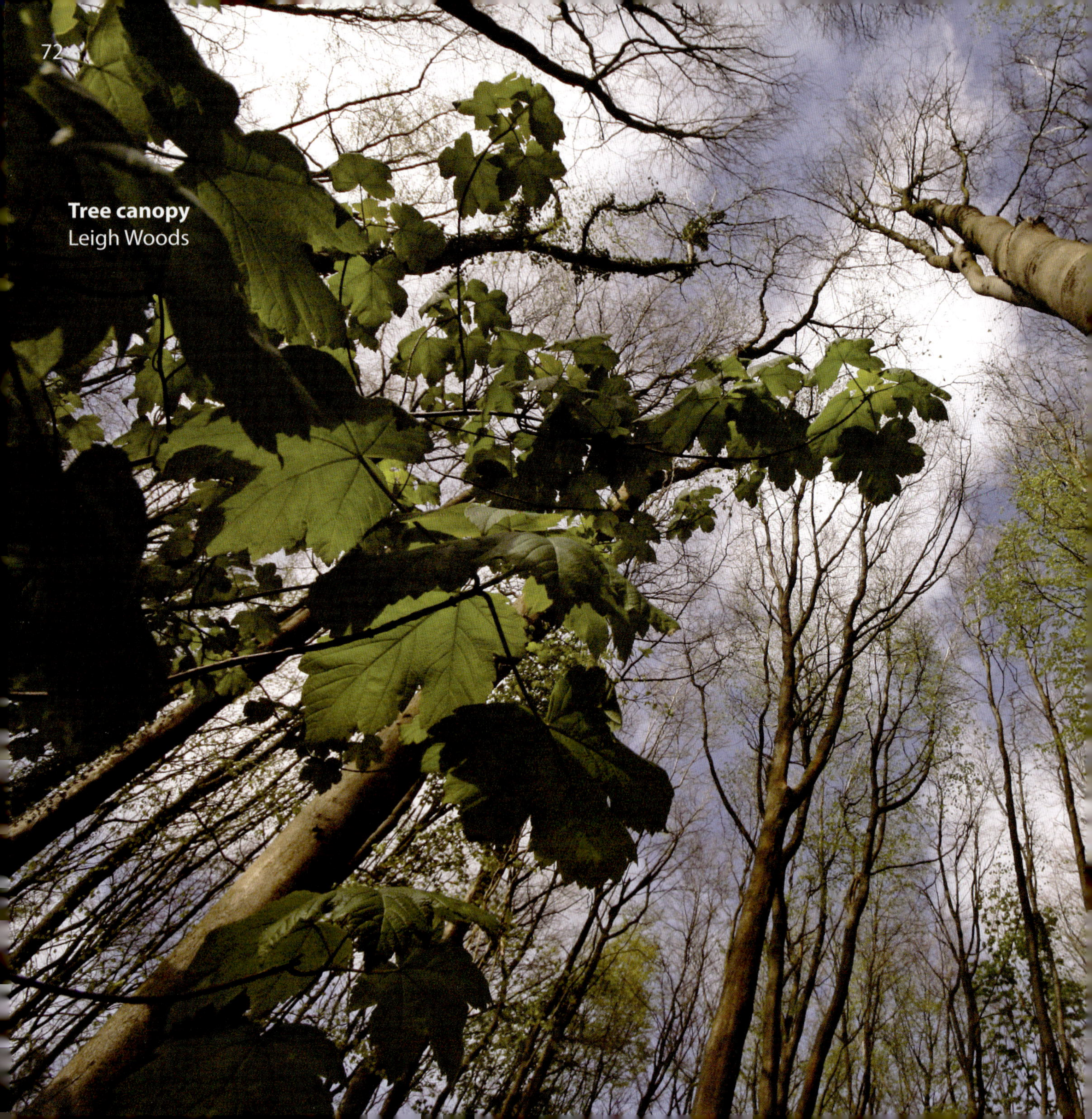
Tree canopy
Leigh Woods

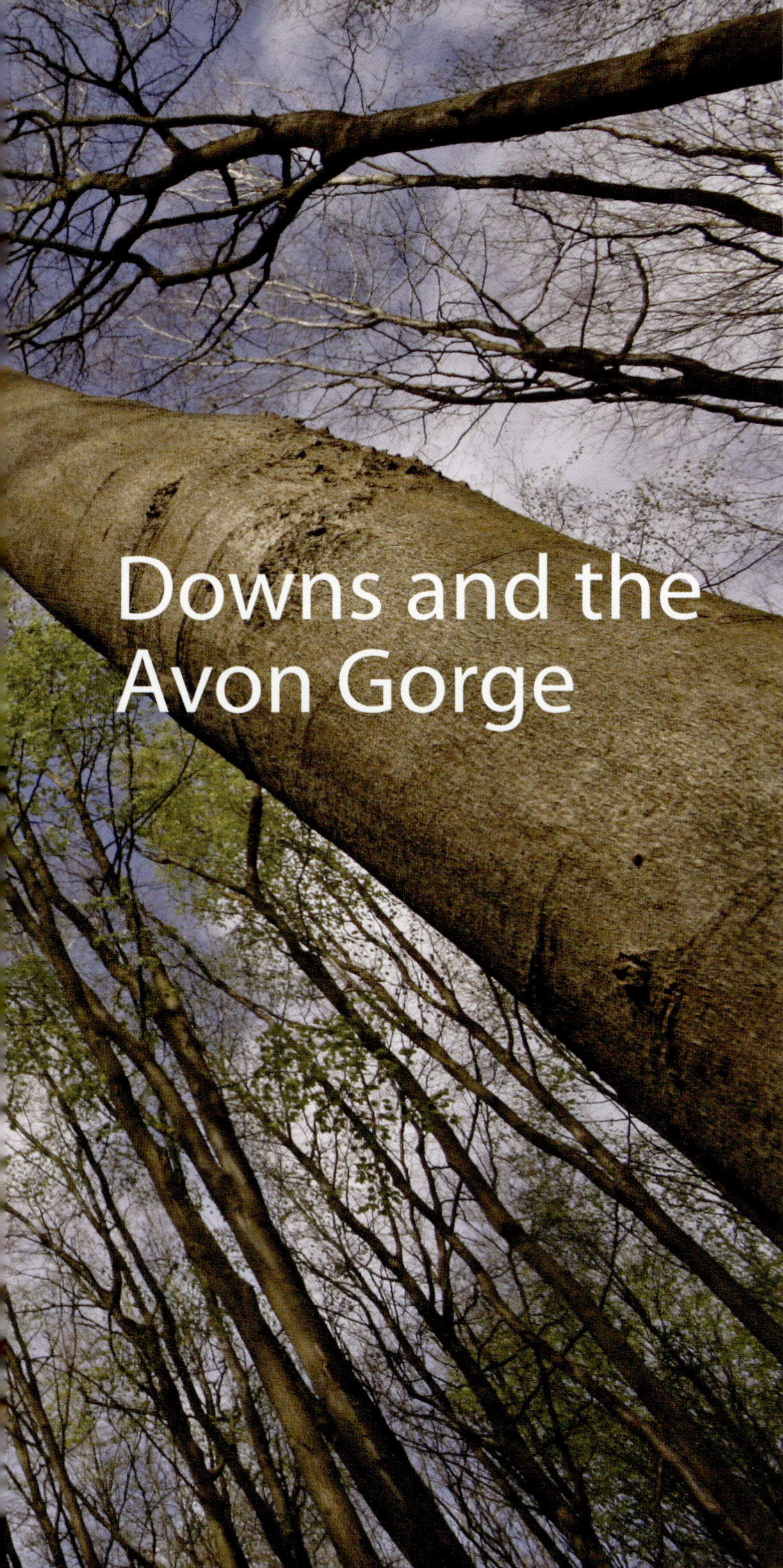

Downs and the Avon Gorge

Although surrounded by the city, the Downs feel like open countryside. The Downs, which run along the eastern edge of the Avon Gorge, are important for wildlife with large areas of limestone grassland brimming with wild flowers. It's also a great place for bird-watching, over 65 different species have been seen here.

The popular robin is mainly associated with the winter months, but this bird lives in the UK all year around. For such a small bird it has a magnificent song which it is joy to hear any morning in Bristol. If you have ever wondered why you can hear robins singing at night it is because the street lights are so bright the bird is fooled into thinking it is day time.

Robin
(Erithacus rubecula)
Robin looking for food during a cold snap on Clifton Downs

Common Bluebell
(Hyacinthoides non-scripta)
Leigh Woods

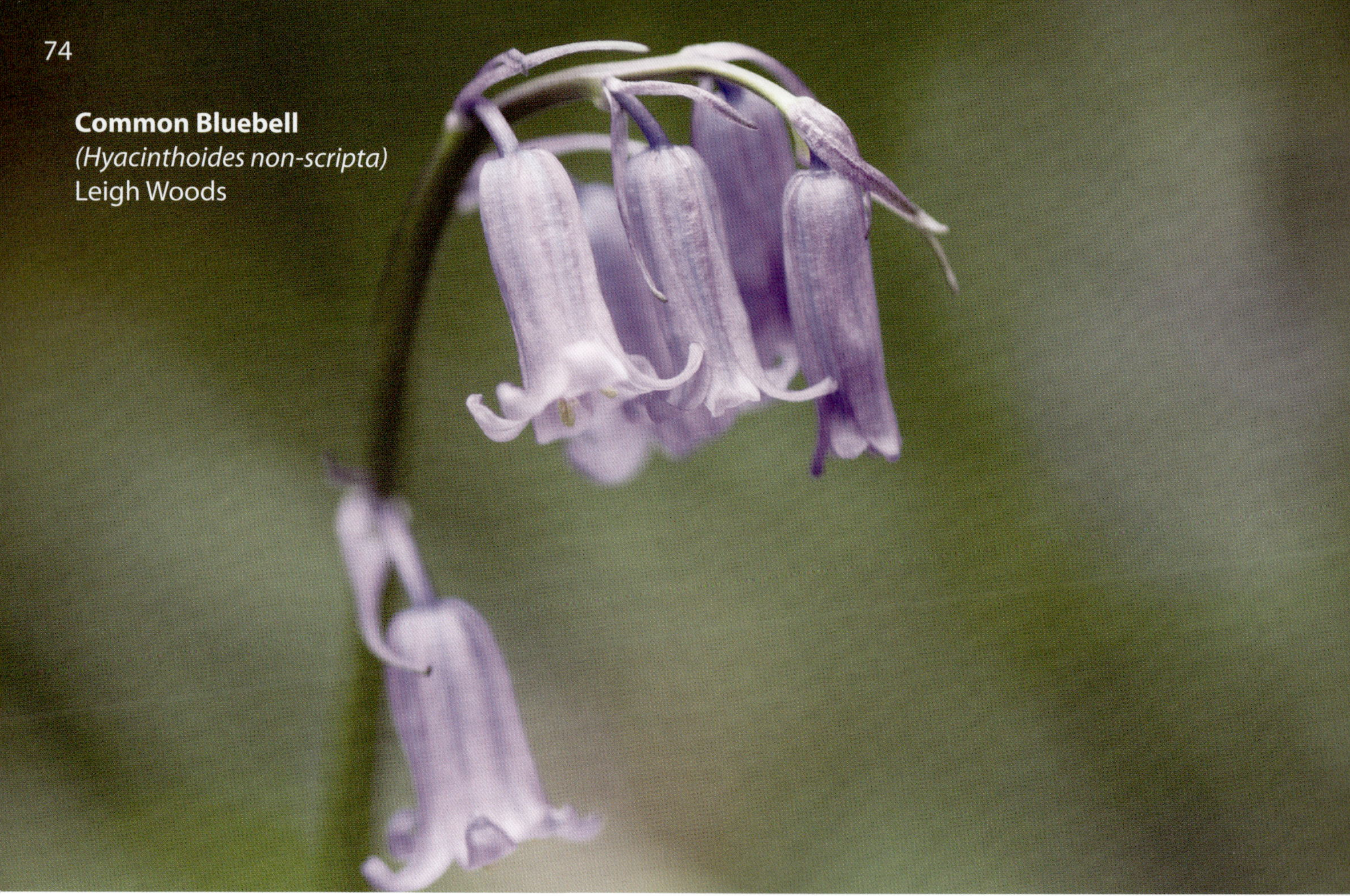

Of the many animals which live on the Downs the ones I see most frequently are red foxes. They leave their earths in the early evening and start heading into the city to scavenge for food, returning again in the early morning. An animal which has been reported to live on the Downs, but I have never seen, is the roe deer. These animals have been reported by early-morning walkers and runners.

The Downs are the perfect habitat for hedgehogs. These funny little animals are great to watch. They are well known for rolling into a ball as a defence mechanism, using their spines to protect themselves. I've read that hedgehogs can communicate in a variety of different ways, including grunts, snuffles, and loud squeals. Keep a look out for hedgehogs especially in autumn as they commonly use bonfires and wood piles as places to hibernate, so be careful not to incinerate one.

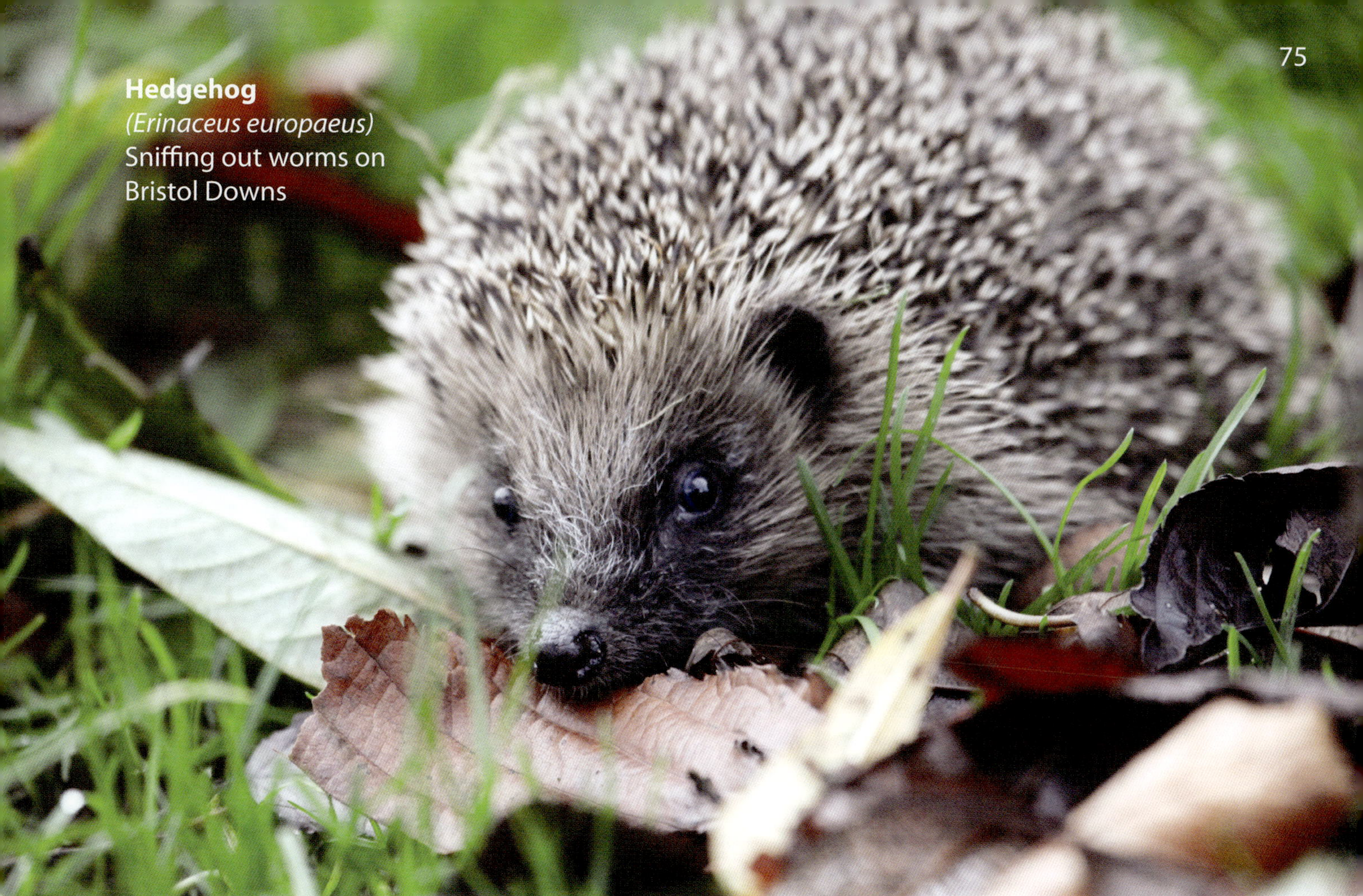

In summer the meadow areas of the Downs are brimming with colour from the many different plants and flowers which grow here: ox-eye daisy, scabious, harebell and wild thyme. You can also find insects in great numbers in the meadows where 21 different species of butterfly have been counted – that's impressive especially for an area so near the city centre. Bristol has given its name to three rare plants. The Bristol onion, Bristol rock cress and Bristol whitebeam are all found in the Avon Gorge and do not grow anywhere else in Britain.

Also living in the Gorge are peregrine falcons. They nearly became extinct in the UK in the 1960s because of widespread pesticide use and illegal killing.

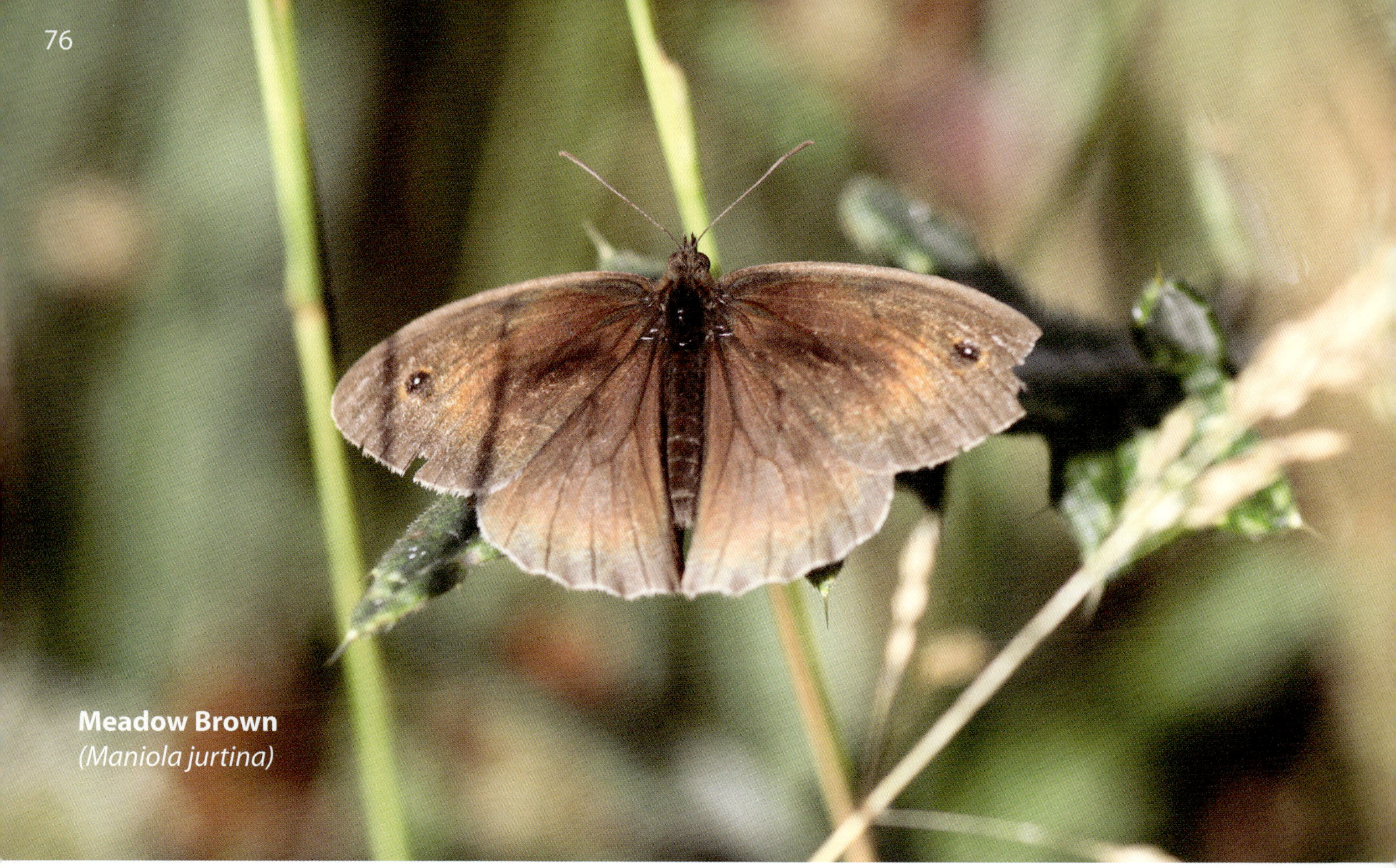

Meadow Brown
(Maniola jurtina)

The Downs are home to 15 different species of tree. One of my favourites is the sycamore. These trees on the Downs are thought to have grown up amongst Brunel's building materials stored here whilst the Suspension Bridge was being constructed. Near the end of the beech avenue on your left you can see a beautiful English oak, planted in 1903 to commemorate the coronation of Edward VII.

The horse chestnut tree has to be the favourite amongst young children as they search for conkers in September. Those on the Downs are believed to have been brought here from the Balkans in the sixteenth century.

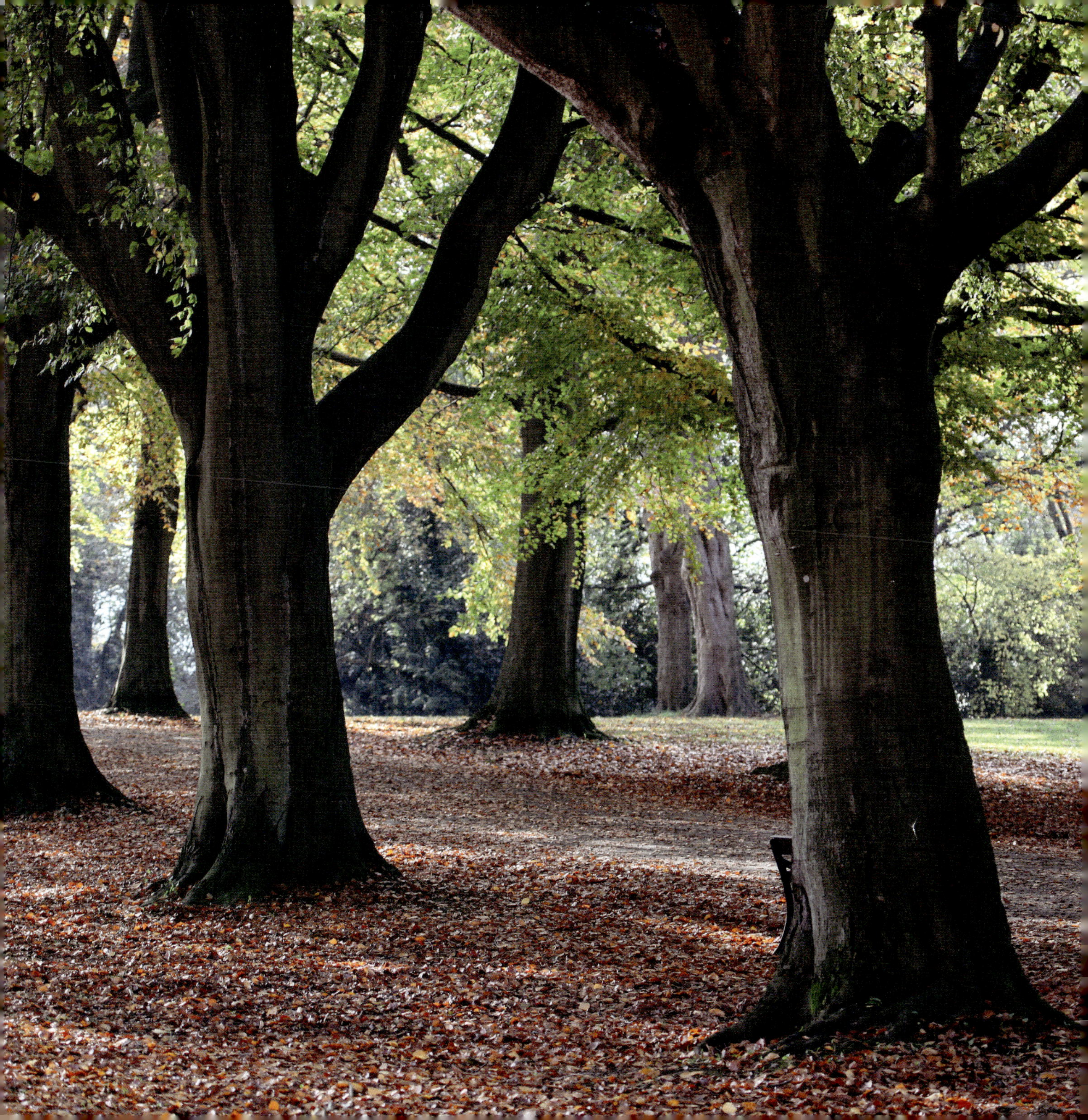

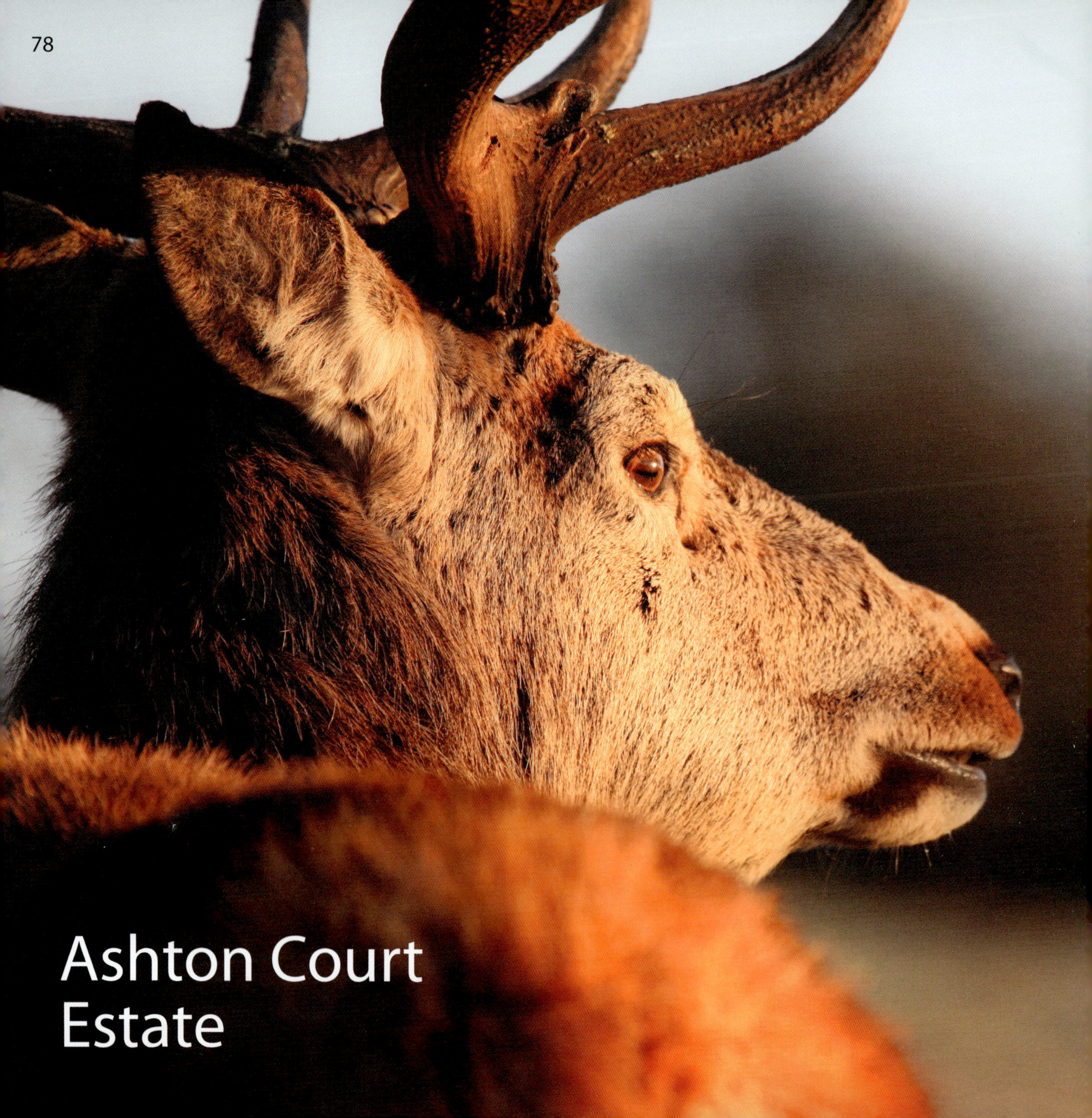
Ashton Court
Estate

Two miles from the centre of Bristol, Ashton Court Estate remains almost entirely surrounded by Somerset countryside.

The estate is about 850 acres of woodland and meadows and has herds of fallow and red deer in special enclosures. The red deer live in the area near the Bower Ashton site of the University of the West of England and the fallow deer live near the House car park. October is a good time to visit the red deer enclosure because it is the start of the rutting season.

The rut is a period when the strongest and biggest male stags round up the females, the hinds, for mating. Males bellow out an echoing roar to maintain control over their group of females and frighten away other males. Visit the red deer enclosure in autumn and you can witness this fantastic spectacle first hand.

Red Deer
(Cervus elaphus)
Autumn sunrise in Red Deer
Park at Ashton Court

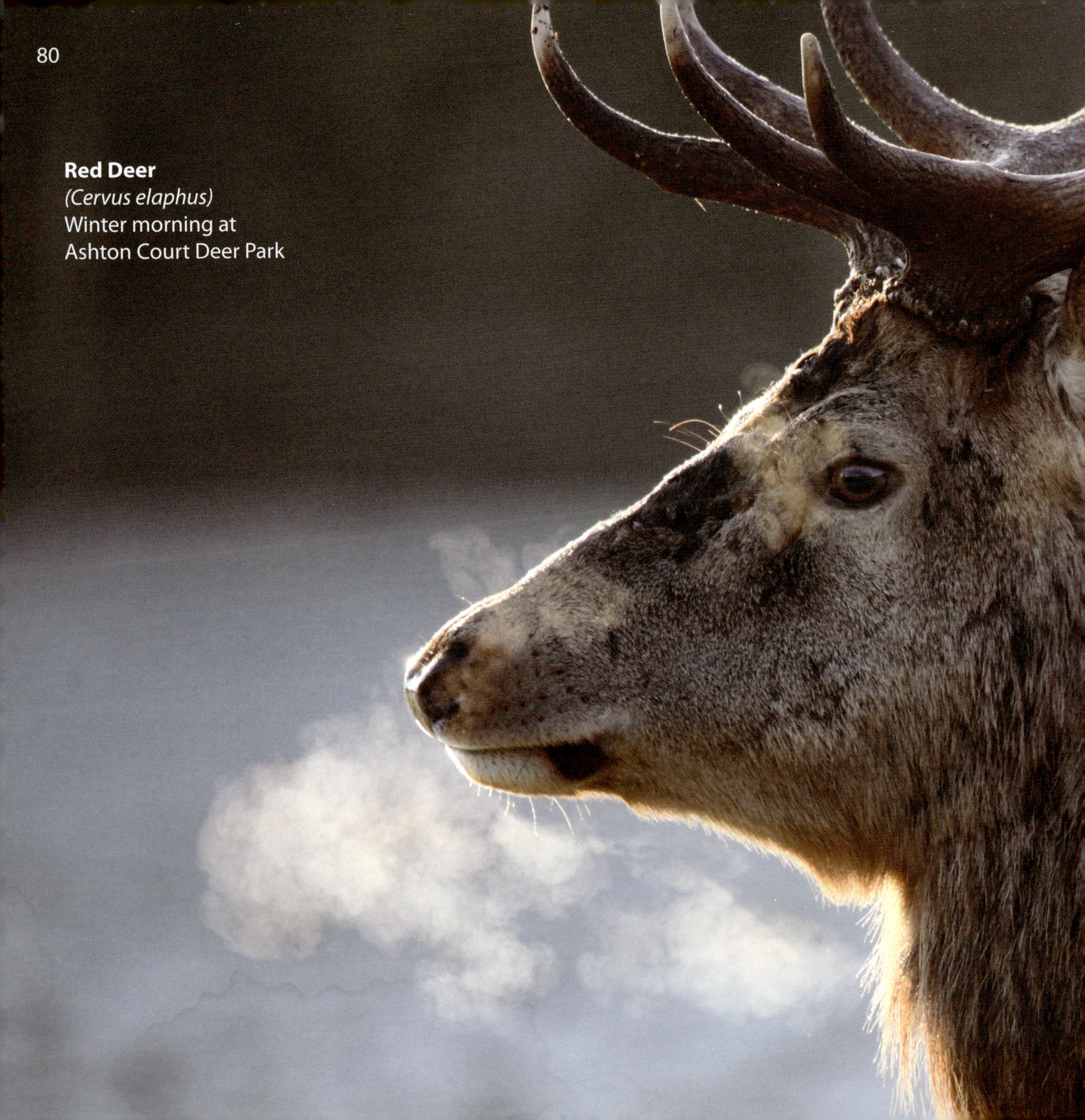

Red Deer
(Cervus elaphus)
Winter morning at
Ashton Court Deer Park

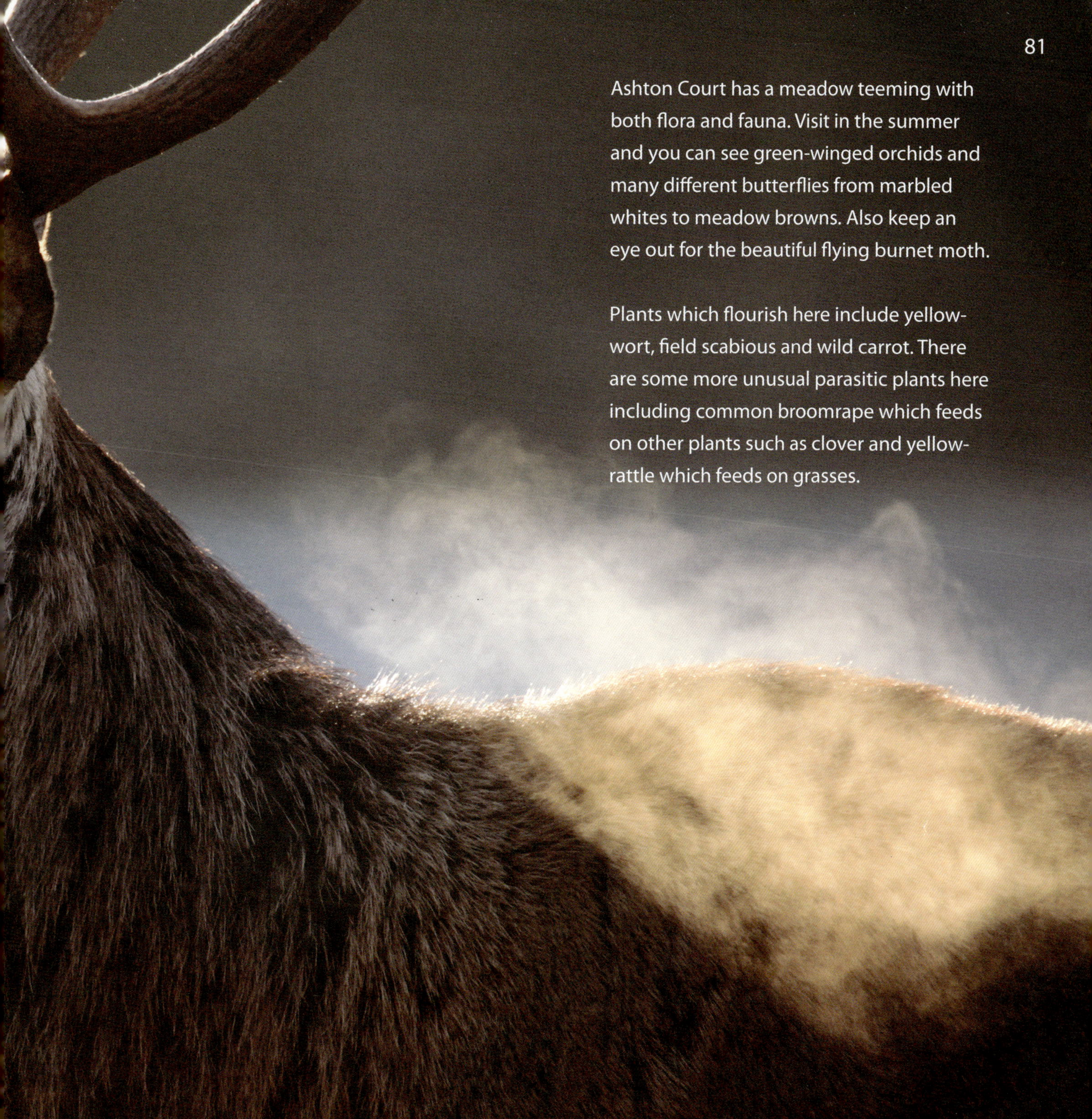

Ashton Court has a meadow teeming with both flora and fauna. Visit in the summer and you can see green-winged orchids and many different butterflies from marbled whites to meadow browns. Also keep an eye out for the beautiful flying burnet moth.

Plants which flourish here include yellow-wort, field scabious and wild carrot. There are some more unusual parasitic plants here including common broomrape which feeds on other plants such as clover and yellow-rattle which feeds on grasses.

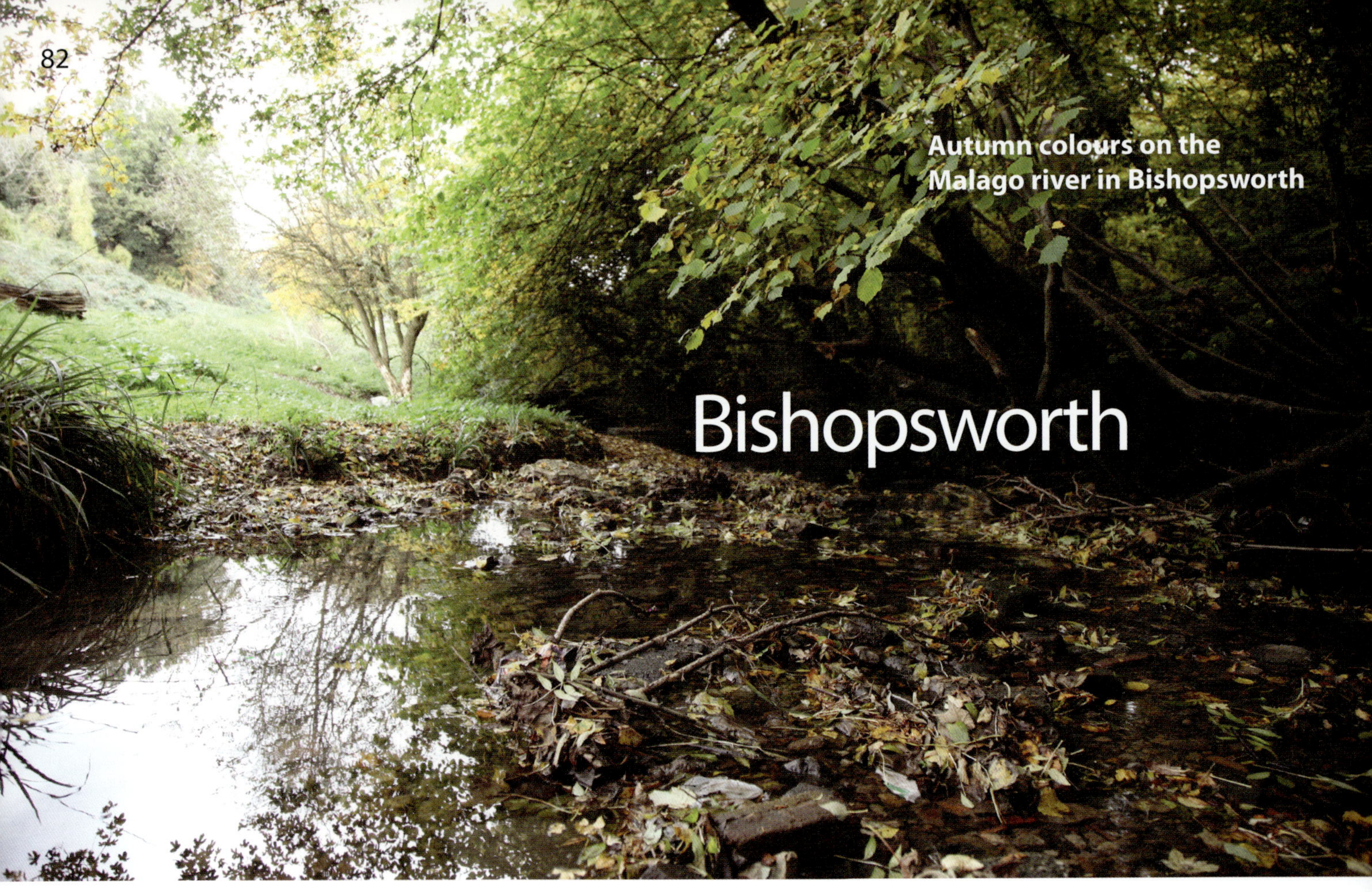

Bishopsworth

Where the Malago river runs through Bishopsworth is an excellent example of how a small wooded area with a stream right in the centre of a busy city can be an oasis of tranquillity and nature. Manor Woods once belonged to the Manor of Bishopsworth and takes its name from the old manor house.

The biggest and most impressive trees in this wood are the majestic oaks. They were probably planted here around 300 years ago. These oaks provide shelter and food for countless different species of insect. After dark you can hear tawny owls calling to each other. Wood mice and other rodents share this rich haven for wildlife.

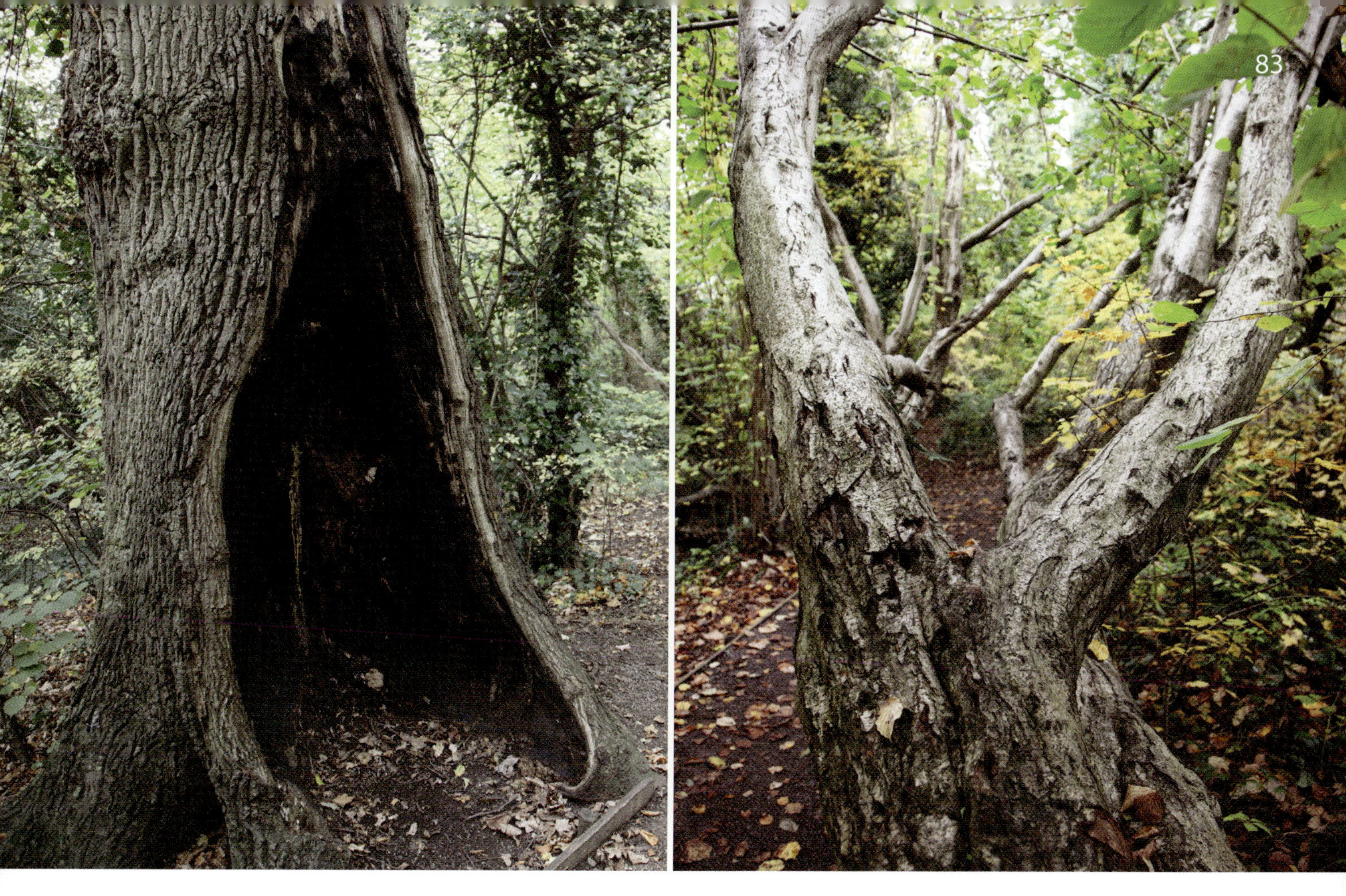

The best time to visit is spring and autumn. In spring you will see a blanket of white flowers, with the strong smell of wild garlic. The woods start to come alive with the sounds of birds like the tiny wren and lovely robin.

Autumn is another great time of year as the leaves start changing to beautiful yellows and oranges filling the woods with cascades of autumnal colour. Mushrooms and toadstools appear in these later months, some growing off trees and others from the soil under foot. Hazelnuts provide ample food for the many grey squirrels which live here.

Bristol City Centre and Stokes Croft

Starlings
(Sturnus vulgaris)
Roosting near Bristol Bridge

Bristol City Centre is also known as the business district. It may look on the outside void of natural life but animals go about their daily business in the skies and in trees and at street level. The Welsh Back area has a large collection of mute swans always on the lookout for food. If you're lucky you can see these huge birds take off and fly out over the city. The sound they make whilst taking off and landing shows the power behind these large birds. Bristol used to have a large starling roost over the city especially over Colston Hall and Bristol Bridge. They have all but gone now but a small roost can be seen in the winter months over Bristol Bridge. After dark the scavengers come out, red foxes which are plentiful in Bristol patrol the streets, looking for leftover food from discarded takeway wrappers and food left in waste bins. Large numbers of rats join in.

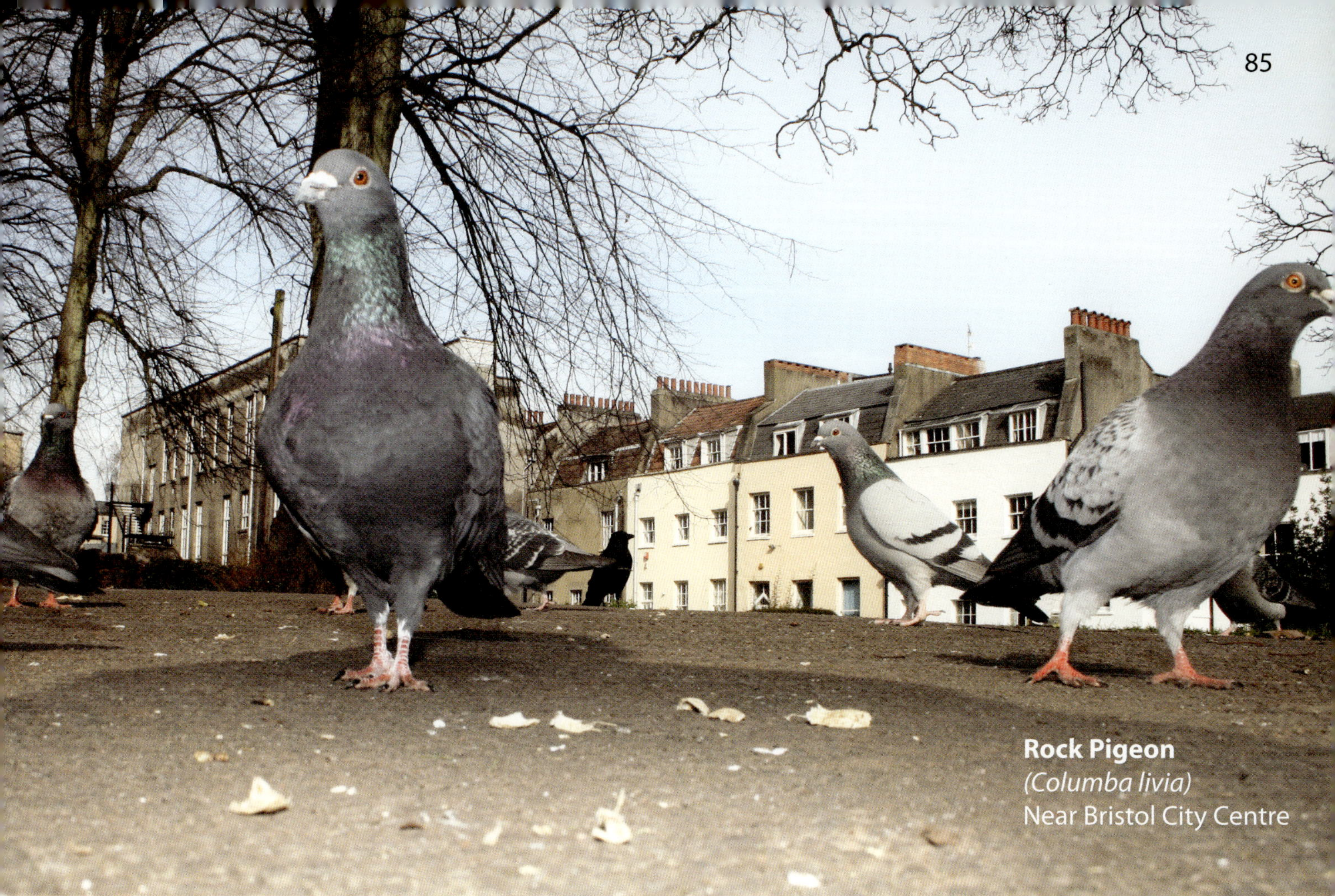

People think of the feral pigeon as a pest and a bird which carries disease. But pigeons are intelligent and have a set routine which ensures their survival. I often think pigeons get a bad rap. They are actually quite beautiful. Few birds in Britain have so much colour variation in their plumage, and when the light catches the bird just right you will see metallic greens, purples and pinks. They love Bristol and most cities because of all the ledges: their equivalent of cliff and rock faces in the countryside. These birds have truly adapted to our cities and the next time you are out in Bristol take a few minutes to look at this pretty, intelligent and adaptable bird.

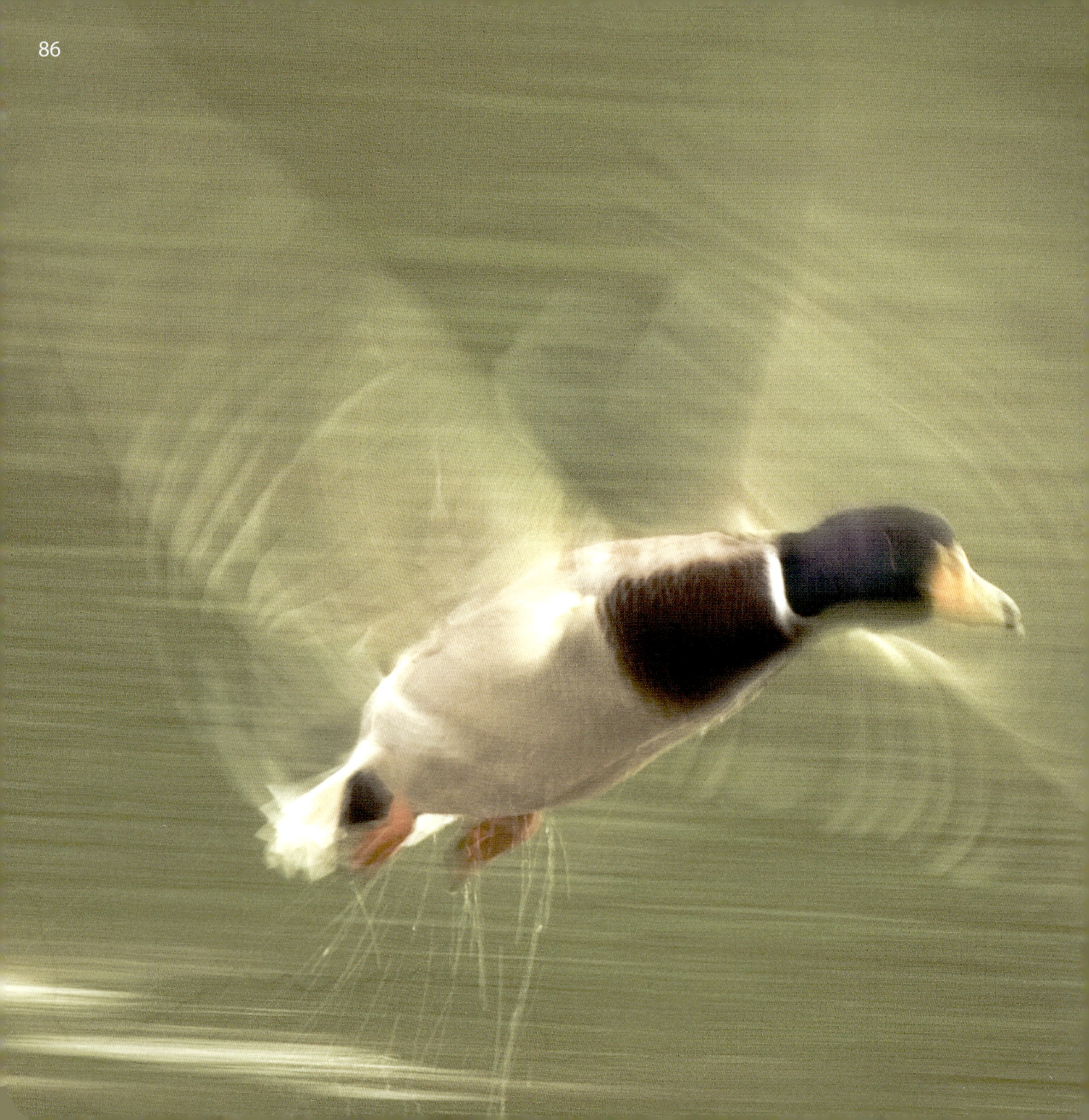

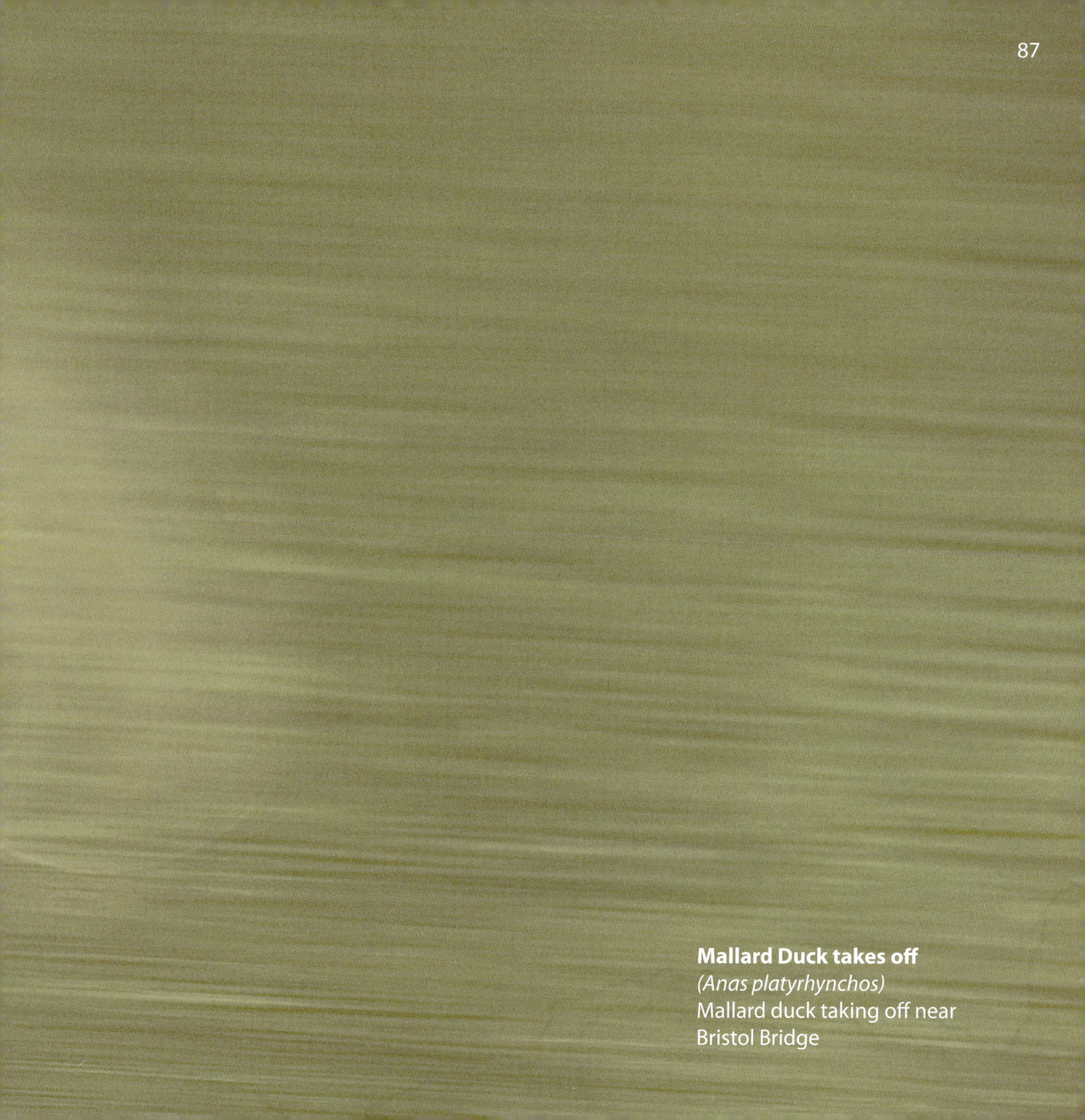

Mallard Duck takes off
(Anas platyrhynchos)
Mallard duck taking off near
Bristol Bridge

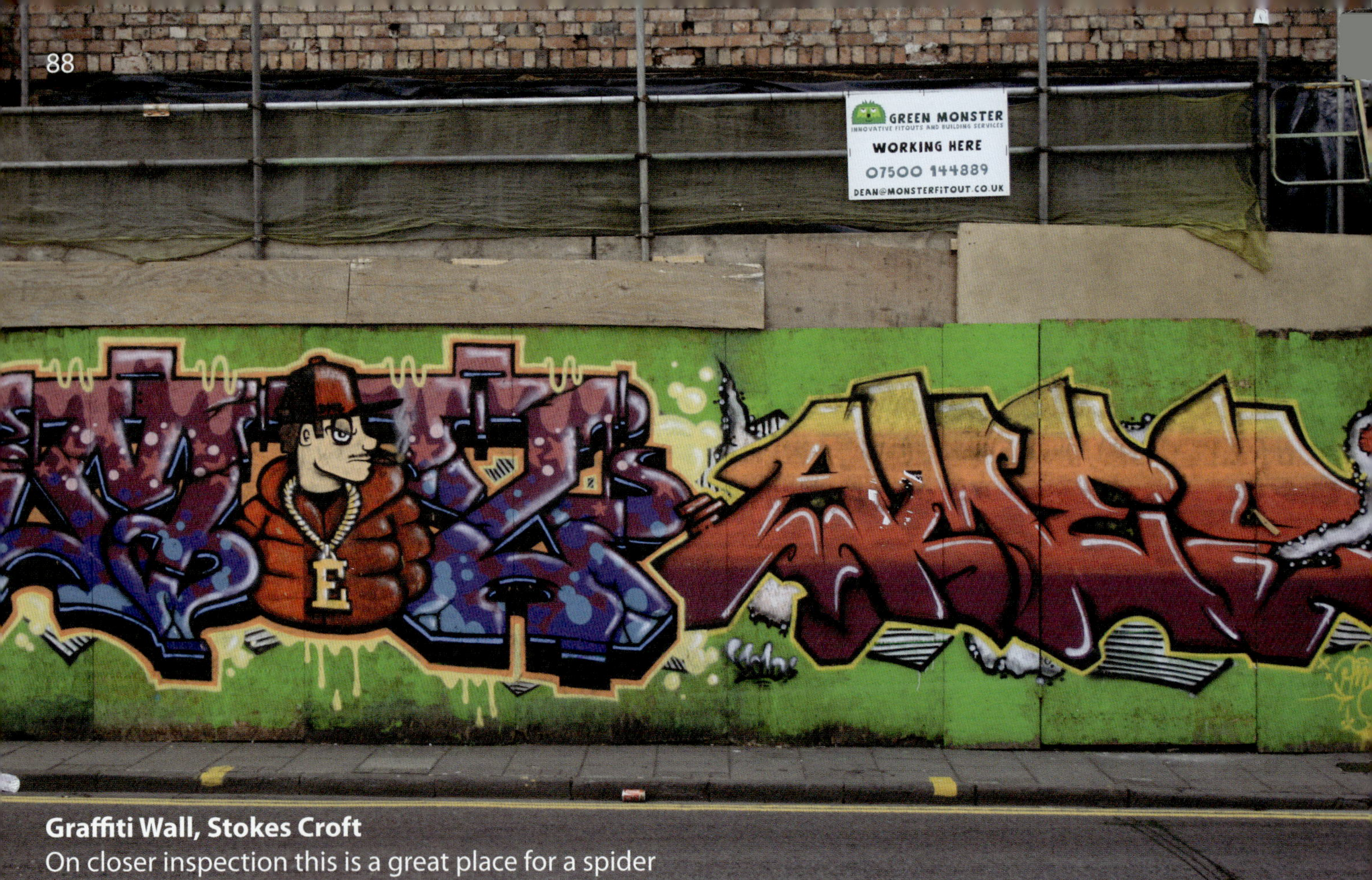

Graffiti Wall, Stokes Croft
On closer inspection this is a great place for a spider

At first glance you would think this area would be devoid of wildlife, but on closer inspection it's a great place for small animals like spiders, woodlice and many other insects feeding or living in or on this wooden surface. Woodlice need moisture so an area like the one pictured above would be perfect. They are usually found in any damp or rotting wood environment. They need damp areas because they breathe through their gills. They can roll up into an almost perfect sphere as a defensive mechanism which is key to survival for a small animal like this. The empty building behind this could be home to many spiders. It may come as a surprise, but a dozen or so species of spider resident in the UK are capable of causing a significant or unpleasant bite. So watch out next time you see a spider.

European Garden Spider
(Araneus diadematus)
Spider using its web to catch flies

European garden spider webs are built by the larger females who usually lie head down on the web, as in this photograph, waiting for prey to get entangled. The prey is then quickly captured and wrapped in silk before being eaten. There are about 600 species of spider in the British Isles, all of which are carnivorous. They have six different types of silk glands or spinnerets located at the rear of the abdomen. Four of them produce different silks depending on their purpose. The other two produce a sticky liquid to aid entrapment of the prey. The individual threads of silk range from 0.03mm to 0.15mm thick and have a similar strength to an equivalent strand of steel. As I was photographing these spiders small objects would blow into the web. The spider would investigate and once it had realised the object was not food it would fling it out.

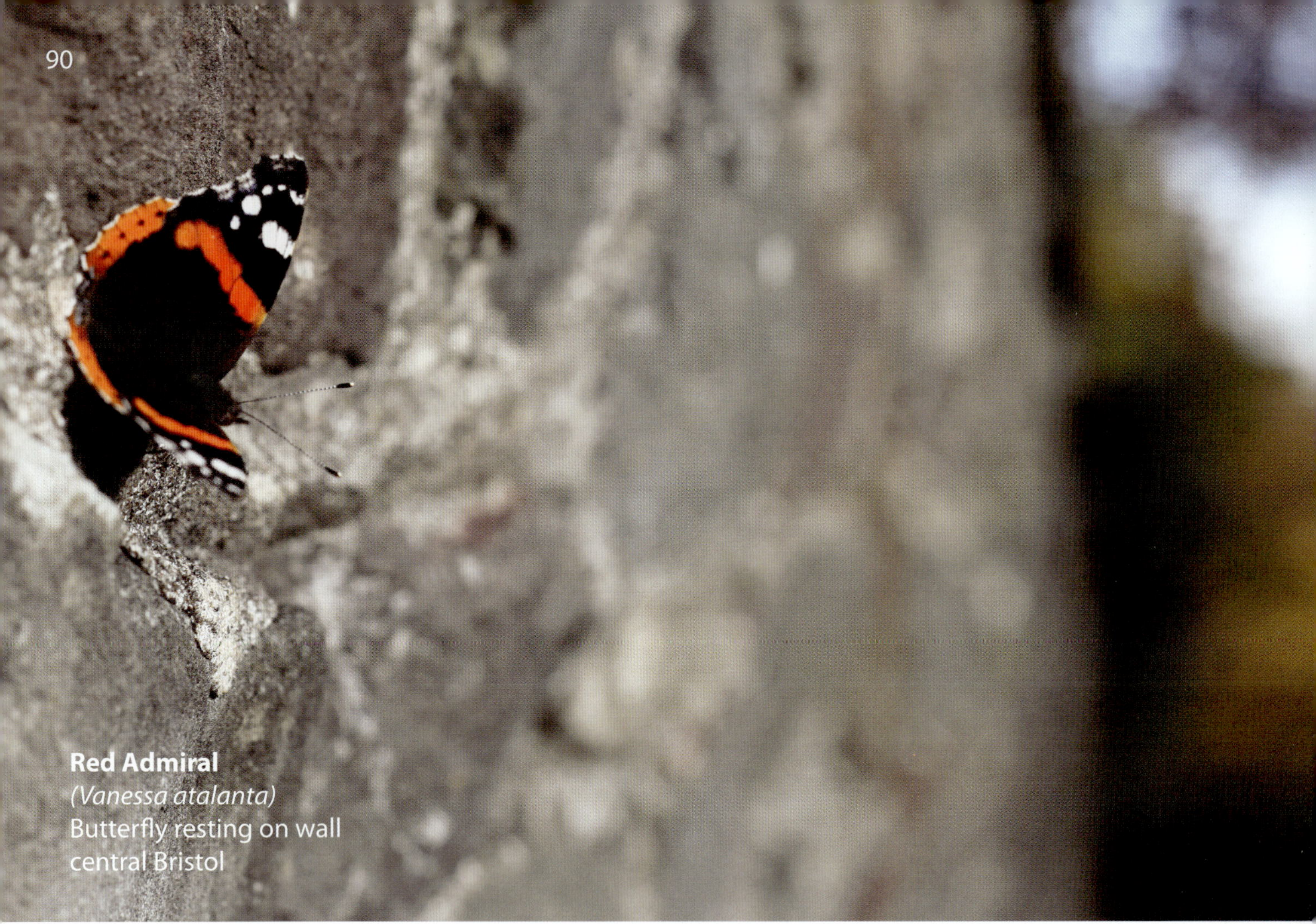

Red Admiral
(Vanessa atalanta)
Butterfly resting on wall
central Bristol

Not far from the city centre in part of the university campus, an eagle owl was living in a tree. It became a local celebrity and was named Oscar. It is believed that he escaped or was released from a private collection and made his home in Bristol. In 2009 he was found dead having – it is believed – eaten a poisoned rat. But it just goes to show how urban environments can became a home to the biggest and the smallest creatures in the animal kingdom.

Bristol - *Connecting with nature*

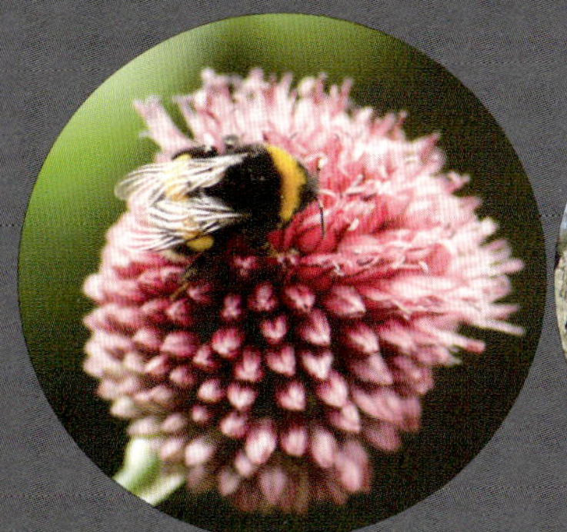

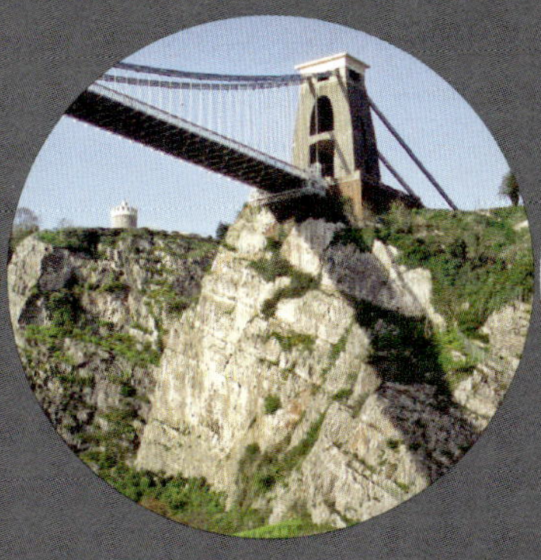

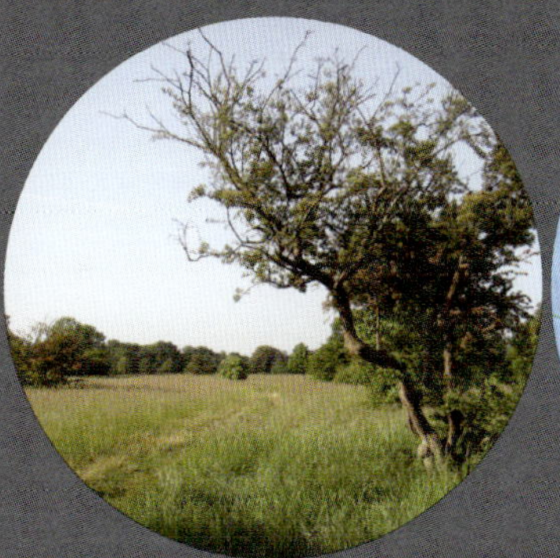

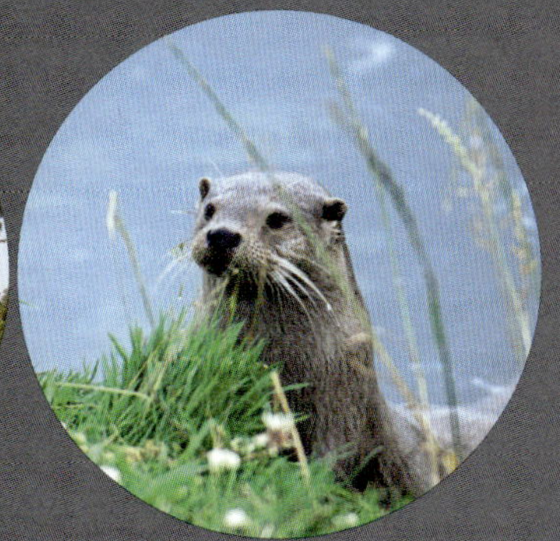

Bristol has rare plants named after it. Bristol Onion, Bristol Rock cress and Bristol Whitebeam are all found in the Avon Gorge and no where else in Britain.

Bristol has an amazing 87 sites of importance for wildlife.

Otters live in the Floating Harbour.

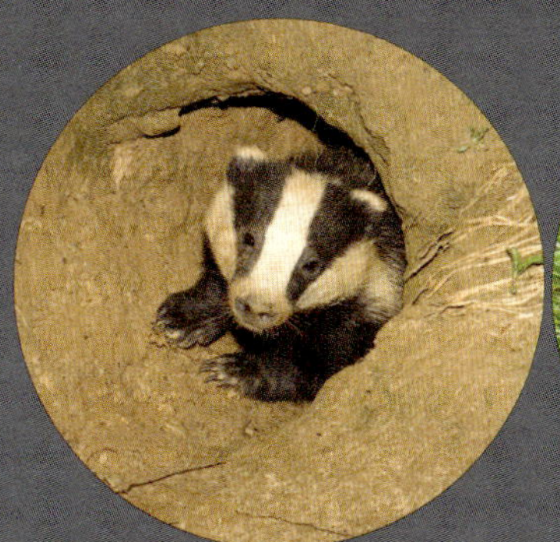

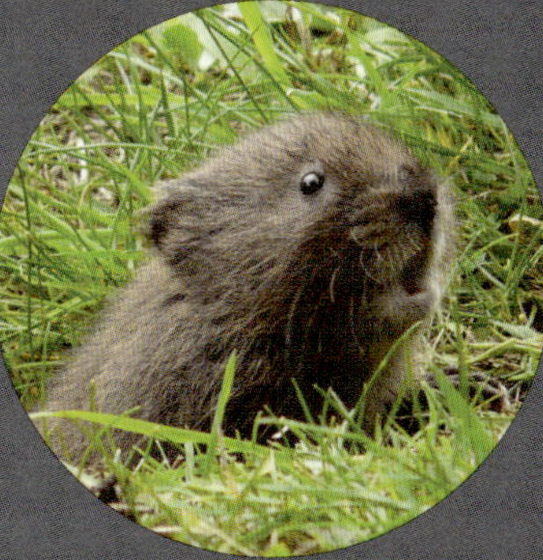

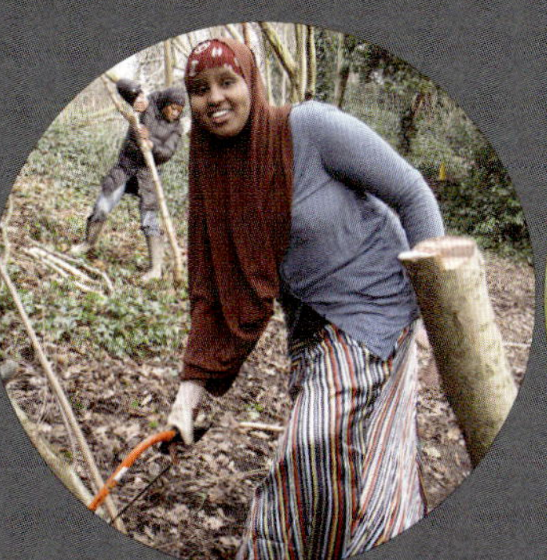

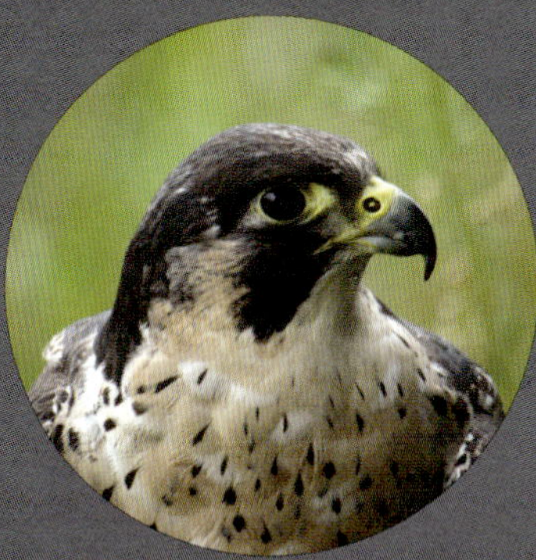

One of the largest badger populations of any city in the UK.

Important population of water voles living in ditches at Avonmouth.

40 groups connecting communities with nature.

Peregrines nest in the Avon Gorge.

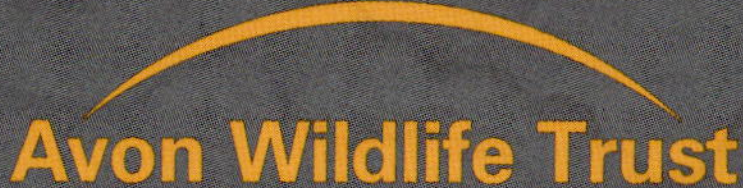

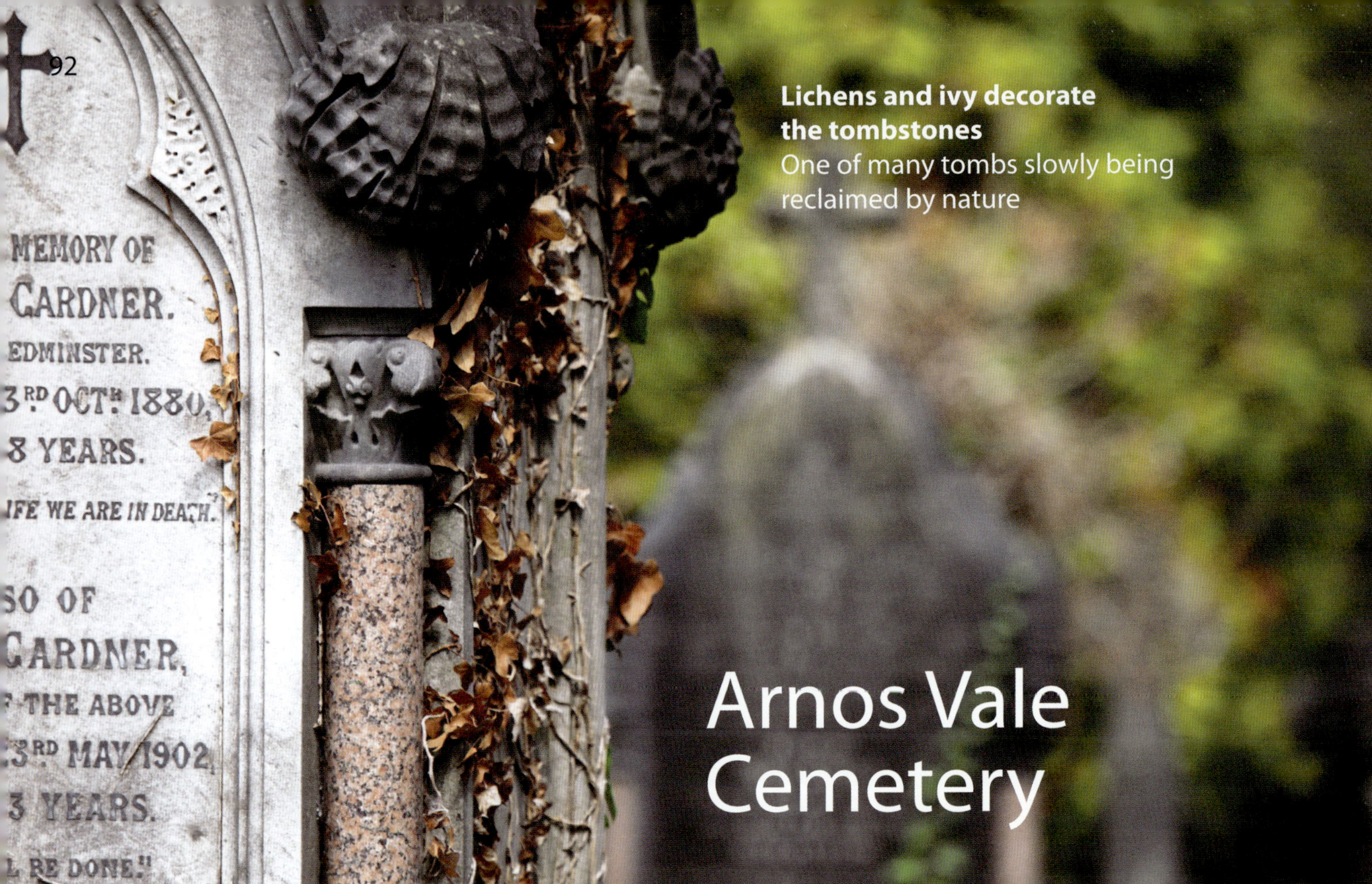

Arnos Vale Cemetery

Arnos Vale Cemetery is a 45-acre haven of peace and quiet in an otherwise busy part of a bustling city. It is a great place for wildlife where many fascinating wild plants and creatures thrive, adding to the enjoyment and interest of visitors and providing wildlife with an essential green corridor that helps an abundance of species to survive in the city. Exploring Arnos Vale reveals wildlife surprises at all times of the year. In spring, there's a vibrant array of wildflowers and the air is full of bird song; in summer, rare migrants can often be heard or glimpsed, while bats put on aerial acrobatics shows; autumn sees brambles heavy with fruit and squirrels laying in food for the winter; as leaves fall and the colder weather starts, the swish of a fox's tail may be spotted and the holly and the ivy show their Yuletide colours. And there is even an Indian notable buried here too.

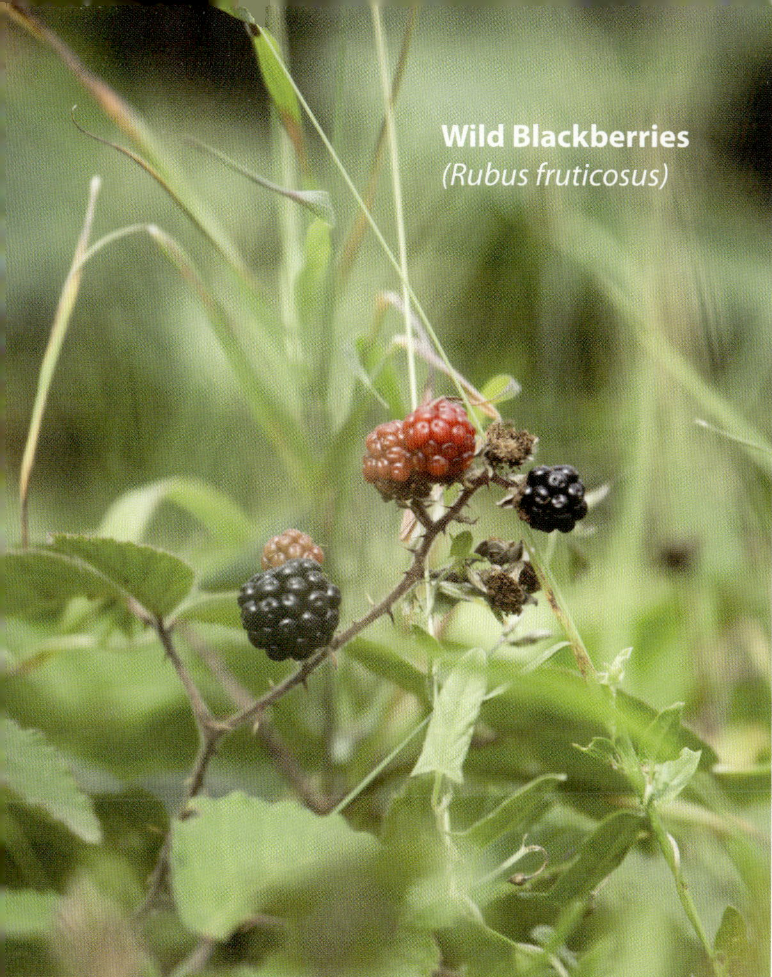

Wild Blackberries
(Rubus fruticosus)

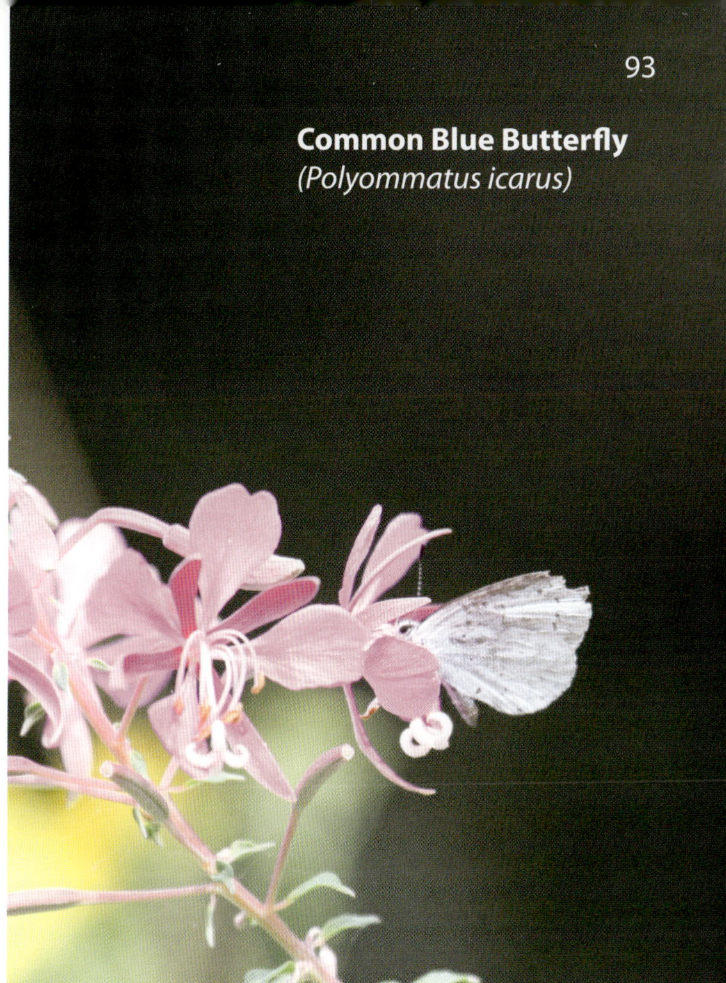

Common Blue Butterfly
(Polyommatus icarus)

The cemetery is registered as a Site of Nature Conservation Interest (SNCI) and is being managed for wildlife. The landscape management plan focuses on conserving the existing grassland and woodland habitats and improving their quality to benefit wildlife.

It is a great place to hear and see visiting and resident birds, as returning warblers nest alongside woodpeckers, thrushes and finches. Firecrest and woodcock find shelter in the winter and other rare migrants such as pied flycatchers and redstarts stop off to refuel on their long journeys in spring and autumn. Slow-worms like the long grass, lichens decorate the tombstones and, at night, bats feed over the trees whilst badgers and foxes forage. Truly a paradise for wildlife.

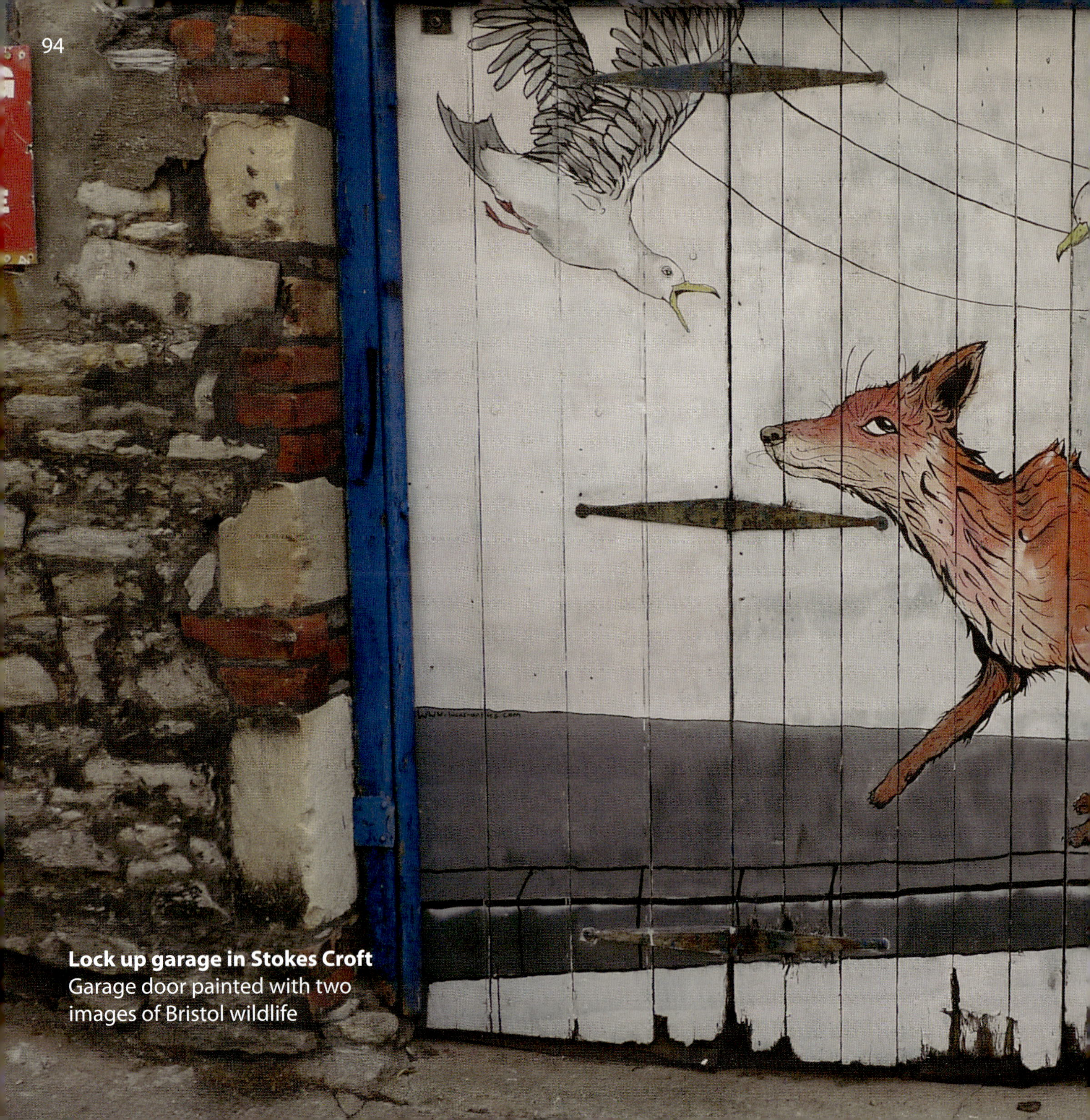

Lock up garage in Stokes Croft
Garage door painted with two
images of Bristol wildlife

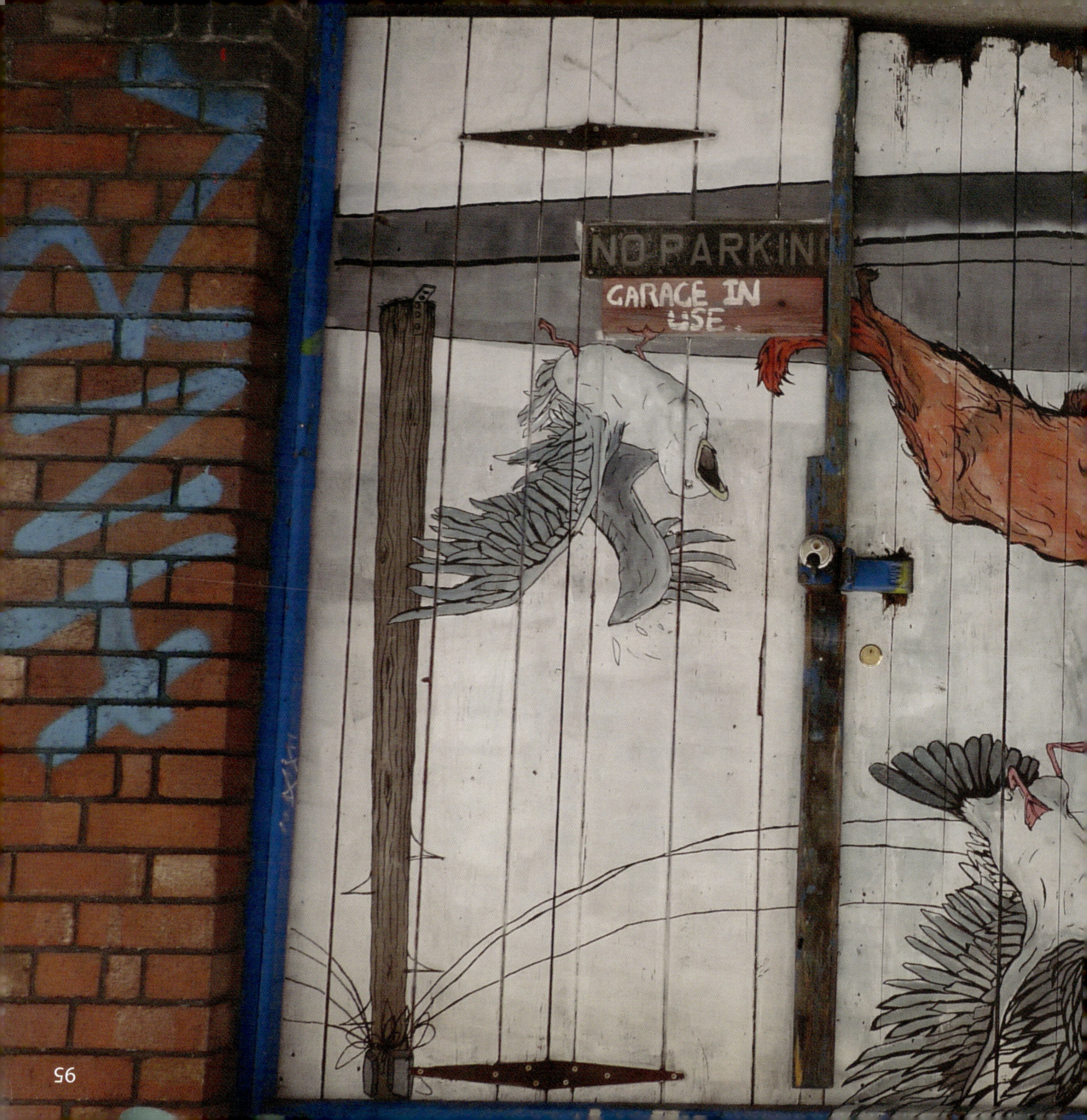

NO PARKING
GARAGE IN USE

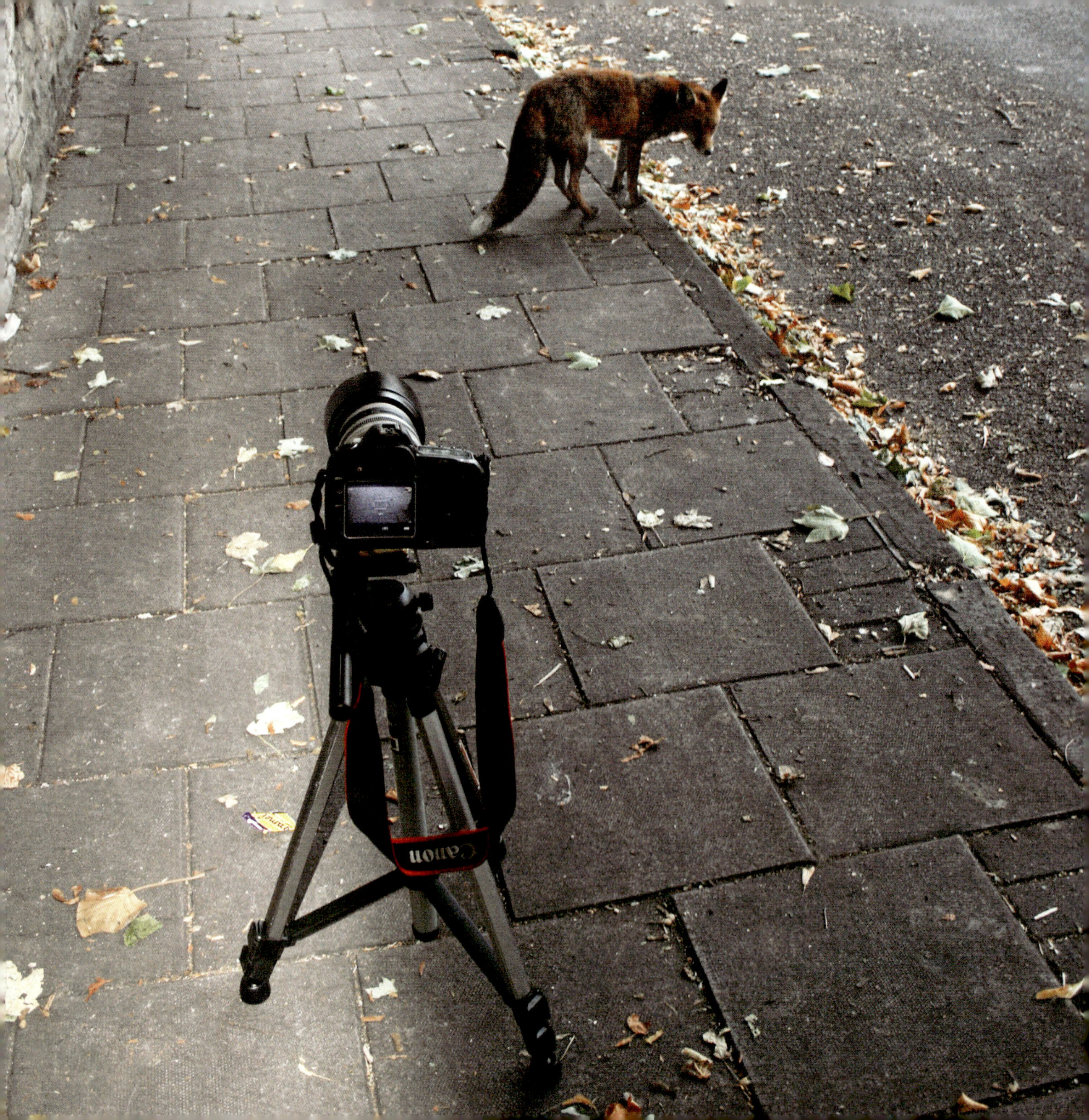

Canon